THE
BLYTH & TYNE
BRANCH

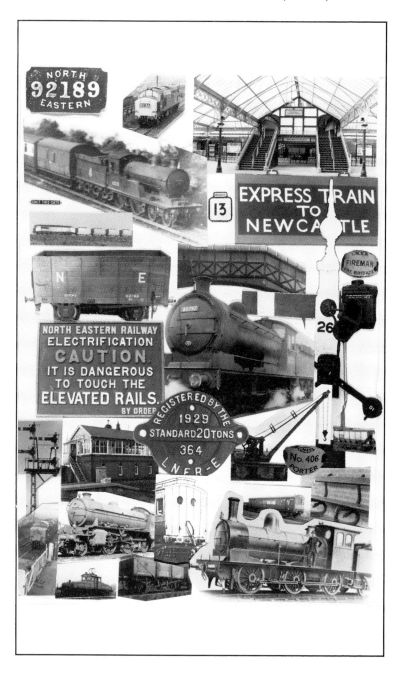

BLYTH & TYNE
PART II

THE
BLYTH & TYNE
BRANCH
1874 - 1989

J A WELLS

First published in 1990 by Northumberland County Library,
The Willows, Morpeth, Northumberland NE61 1TA.

Copyright © J A Wells and Northumberland County Library 1990

Printed by Printers Inc Ltd., Newcastle upon Tyne

British Library Cataloguing in Publication Data
Wells, J A (James Alan)
The Blyth & Tyne Branch, 1874 — 1989
Blyth & Tyne part II
1. North-East England. Railway services, history
I. Title
385. 09428

ISBN 0-9513027 5 2

Contents

List of Illustrations

List of Maps, Charts, Posters and Diagrams

Preface

NO OTHER RAILWAY has a history that compares with the Blyth & Tyne Branch in Northumberland.

Its origins were the Blyth & Tyne Railway Company whose territory included Bedlington, Blyth, Morpeth, Newcastle upon Tyne, Percy Main and Tynemouth, a notable achievement in itself considering it all started from colliery railways as far back as 1840. Before that, Bedlington had a waggonway to the River Blyth in 1609, one of the earliest in the country. The Iron Works there not only manufactured railway lines from 1820 for use in many parts of the country but also produced good quality locomotives.

Some of George Stephenson's early 'iron horses' worked on the Killingworth waggonway, or were tested there, on a line crossed by the Blyth & Tyne since 1864.

From 1874, when it became part of the North Eastern Railway, the volume of coal carried on the Branch increased dramatically. In 1961 Blyth was Europe's busiest coal port, handling nearly seven million tons. The NER designed and built several classes of smart and very efficient engines to work this traffic some of which continued in use until the end of steam on British Railways.

A major milestone in passenger traffic was the introduction of electric trains on the Branch between Newcastle and Tynemouth in 1904, the first in Great Britain. Subsequently this same route became part of the Tyneside Metro, the first rapid, light transit system in the United Kingdom.

Inevitably times change and the Branch has reflected this, being much reduced in size and complexity by 1989. There are no passenger trains now as the Metro does not belong to British Rail. Stations and sidings have gone but coal in full train loads is still carried, together with alumina and aluminium. Nevertheless, from 1990 some steam-hauled trains will operate from the Stephenson Museum centre to Percy Main along the former Blyth & Tyne route.

This book traces the fascinating story of the Branch over the 115 years since 1874. It shows the development of passenger, mineral and goods traffic and gives details of stations, motive power depots, signalling and derailments. The book has a special tribute to some of the men who served on the Branch. It also contains information which gives an insight of historical interest into railway working.

I would like to express my sincere gratitude to the following for the assistance they have given me in their various ways during the preparation of this book:—

Blyth Harbour Commissioners and Mr D W Hetherington:

British Alcan, Lynemouth and Mr K Watson:

British Rail - Area Managers - P Atack, K Dickens and G Robson;
            Staff at Morpeth station;
            Public Relations Department:

Newcastle Central Library, Local Studies Section:

North Eastern Railway Association:

North Shields Local Studies Centre staff (Metropolitan Borough of North Tyneside):

Northumberland County Library - Mr. G S Payne, County
                                        Librarian;
            Messrs C Mackenzie and D Bonser;
            Morpeth Office staff;
            Blyth Library staff:

Northumberland County Record Office:

Tyne & Wear Passenger Transport Executive.

Messrs T Allan, G E Charlton, L G Charlton, M Charlton, J C Dean, J M Fleming (President of the North Eastern Railway Association), R Miles, J Nicholson, F Scott, B Simpson, R Steward (Deputy County Archivist), I Story, D W Thornton, D A Wells.

I must give a special word of thanks to my wife, June, for many hours of typing and checking, also for her patience.

Finally, I am very grateful to Northumberland County Library for publishing the second part of *Blyth & Tyne*.

                                                    J. A. WELLS

To the memory of
Andrew and Hilda Turner
and
James E and Eleanor Wells

Chapter 1

Background:
The Blyth & Tyne Railway

THE BLYTH & TYNE RAILWAY COMPANY was formed by Act of
Parliament from 1 January 1853 but the history of this notable branch
line in south-east Northumberland has a pedigree stretching back to
the earliest waggonways in the district. It all started with the rich
seams of *coal* and the line owed its existence to this remarkable and
highly marketable commodity.

Shafts were sunk as near as possible to a navigable river where it
was a comparatively simple task to transfer coal direct to colliers if
the water was deep enough. If not it was taken on board shallow
boats known as *keels* and transferred to the ships in deeper water. As
seams became worked out or uneconomic to mine, collieries were
developed further and further inland and the coal was transported
along *waggonways* using at first the principle of one horse one
waggon. Mining and transporting coal was a labour-intensive but
dangerous industry in those early days. The collieries in Northumberland were at the forefront of waggonway development because at
least one was in use as far back as 1608, leading to the River Blyth
near Bedlington. Wooden rails were used later to guide the wheels
of the *chaldron waggons* but it was only a matter of time before the
flanges on the rails were transferred to the wheels of the waggons and
wood gave way to cast iron, then malleable iron, rails. The Iron Works
at Bedlington were in the vanguard for the production of these rails
which they supplied over a wide area from 1820 onwards: in fact
Michael Longridge, a partner in the firm, worked closely with George
Stephenson.

The demand for coal grew rapidly. It was well known it could be
used to heat water which then turned into steam - but could that steam
be harnessed and used to power machinery? Richard Trevithick
proved it could. Other pioneers such as John Blenkinsopp, William
Chapman, William Hedley, George and Robert Stephenson and
Nicholas Wood developed his ideas and produced railway locomo-

tives in the north east of England destined to have influences world-wide on trade, travel and social development. Railways became the greatest of all industrial legends and were Great Britain's gift to mankind. Stephenson's first locomotive, called *Blucher*, built at Killingworth in 1814, was capable of hauling eight loaded waggons (about thirty tons gross) at walking pace: only eight years later, however, he used one of his engines at the same colliery to demonstrate to visitors how it could haul *twenty* loaded waggons "with the utmost facility".

In 1822/23 considerable amounts of capital were invested in collieries at Seghill and Cramlington. Waggonways to the Tyne were already in use from several pits. One of these was the Backworth waggonway which led to staiths at Hayhole (later called Northumberland Dock). A waggonway to join this one was laid circa 1822 from Cramlington and coal from Seghill was transported by the Cramlington Coal Company over this route. Some years later a line from Seaton Delaval colliery added more traffic, all of which had to pass over the section owned by the Backworth Coal Company. As the number of collieries using the Backworth Waggonway increased so the route became more and more congested, with inevitable delays to the movement of coal.

As a result of this, the Cramlington Coal Company made its own way to the Tyne from 1839. In June of the following year the Seghill Railway was opened thus creating another line to the same river; it also carried the output from Seaton Delaval colliery. Passenger trains ran to Percy Main from Seghill from 28 August 1841. Two locomotives, *Samson* and *John,* both built by Timothy Hackworth, worked as far as Holywell, after which rope haulage from stationary engines was used. From June 1844 their passenger and goods trains were worked by the Newcastle & North Shields Railway.

Hartley harbour (later Seaton Sluice) and Blyth were used as outlets for a considerable quantity of coal from the Northumberland Coalfield but in those days they were shallow and inadequate thus trade was impeded. Collieries in the Blyth and Bedlington area therefore urgently needed rail access to the River Tyne so it is not surprising that the Seghill Railway was extended to New Hartley in 1846 and Blyth in 1847 when it was designated the Blyth, Seghill & Percy Main Railway. Hester Pit, at Hartley, was given a rail connection together with a direct waggonway to Dairy House and thereby to the harbour at Seaton Sluice on a private line. In spite of having to commission a huge wooden viaduct over the River Blyth, 80 feet high and 770 feet in length, the Bedlington Coal Company built a line from a colliery near Bedlington to Newsham, where a connection was made in 1850 with the track to Blyth. Passenger trains were introduced a few weeks later, there being an intermediate station at Cowpen Lane. After some years this was renamed Bebside.

The private companies that shared the railway to the Tyne faced threats of competition from other colliery owners who wanted to construct a separate line to North Shields, where they hoped to build staiths near the mouth of the river. To safeguard themselves the existing companies made an official application in 1851 for powers of incorporation. The Royal Assent for the formation of the Blyth & Tyne Railway Company was given on 30 June 1852, to take effect from 1 January 1853, meanwhile the gradient on Prospect Hill was cut down so that locomotives could be used all the way to Percy Main. At that time the route mileage from there to Blyth was some thirteen miles plus the private section to Bedlington.

To stave off the thrust of rival contenders the Company officials deposited plans for expansion almost immediately which would enable them to extend their route to Morpeth and to Tynemouth. These were approved by Parliament.

In 1854 coke works were erected at Seghill, partly to supply fuel for their locomotives. At the end of that year work started on an engine 'stable' at Percy Main, the centre of operations, together with workshops for the construction and repair of locomotives, coaches and waggons.

Although the route to Morpeth was staked out in the autumn of 1853, construction in earnest did not commence until 1856. The *Official* Opening of the extension for mineral traffic was on 1 October 1857 by which time the Company had bought the Newsham to Bedlington section, sometimes referred to as the Davison Railway. Passenger and goods traffic were introduced the following April, using also the intermediate stations built at Choppington and Hepscott. Percy Main to Morpeth became the Company's main line so the section from Newsham to Blyth was then regarded as a branch. The Blyth and Tyne station at Morpeth was erected alongside the North Eastern Railway's main line station which was built originally by the Newcastle & Berwick Railway in 1847.

In 1859 a junction was made at Bedlington from where the line was taken across the River Wansbeck to North Seaton. Plans to extend this further north were not implemented: instead a terminus was made at Newbiggin-by-the-Sea, though not until 1872.

It was the end of October 1860 before the line was opened between Dairy House (near Hartley) and Tynemouth, part of which was laid along the former Whitley Waggonway. After some delay, passengers and goods were carried from the following April, initially it was only coal. Between Hartley and the Dairy House junction a small halt called The Avenue catered for passengers who wished to visit the grounds and gardens at Seaton Delaval Hall. (Almost certainly the three special trains used to convey people to a large temperance gathering held there in August 1861 used that station.) Before Tynemouth was reached there was Whitley station, sited not far from where Monkseaton Metro now stands. The first Blyth & Tyne station at Tynemouth was situated between what is currently the Master Mariners' Home and the Tynemouth Lodge Hotel. A second, temporary, terminus was used while a third station was being built a little nearer the town - all in a space of five years! When the new station was opened the second one was renamed North Shields; the first became North Shields Terminus. It was later a goods depot. Station number three was placed alongside that of the North Eastern Railway (built originally by the Newcastle & North Shields Railway) and succeeded in taking many passengers from that much bigger Company.

If the NER was one of the Goliaths of the railway world the little Blyth & Tyne certainly tried to be the David! It encroached even further into North Eastern territory by being granted permission to build its own line between Newcastle and Tynemouth. The Newcastle terminus was at New Bridge Street and there were stations at Jesmond, Gosforth, Longbenton, Forest Hall, Hotspur Place, Whitley (on a different site from the original), Cullercoats and North Shields. A halt was provided at Moor Edge for race traffic. Subsequently, Longbenton and Forest Hall were replaced by Benton, and Hotspur Place by Backworth. The line was opened throughout in June 1864.

The Blyth & Tyne Railway followed an aggressive policy of expansion. It was a very progressive Company with its own set of rules and regulations, very efficiency-conscious and seeking always to be cost effective. It ran numerous excursion trains, had traffic agreements with the North British Railway and its associates and always paid good dividends. Its engines were of sturdy, proven designs, while its coaches were transformed in a short time from being what the locals called *bumler boxes* to some of the best in the country at that time. It was the last independent line in the North Eastern Railway area between the Tweed and the Humber.

Finally, in 1874, it did become part of the NER - a thorn in the flesh removed. The Blyth & Tyne Railway became the Blyth & Tyne Branch and through the days of the North Eastern Railway, the LNER and British Railways, right up to the present time, its name has lived on - a fitting tribute.

(For additional information see "Blyth & Tyne Part 1 - The Blyth & Tyne Railway" by the same author, published in 1989 by Northumberland County Library.)

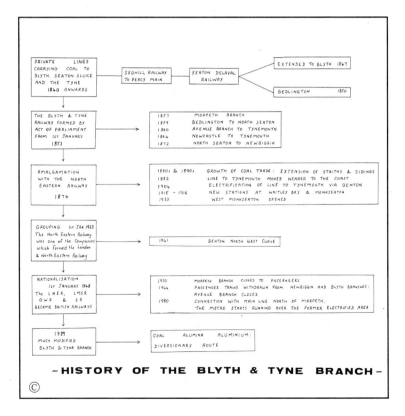

– **HISTORY OF THE BLYTH & TYNE BRANCH** –

Fig. 1

Chapter 2

Developments after 1874

TOWARDS THE END of January 1874 amalgamation terms between the Blyth & Tyne Railway Company and the North Eastern Railway Company were agreed. The Act permitting the merger received the Royal Assent on 7 August of that year.

To summarise the previous chapter, the following routes were acquired by the NER:-

FROM

Percy Main via Prospect Hill and Earsdon Junction to Seghill, Seaton Delaval, Hartley, Newsham, Bebside, Bedlington, Choppington, Hepscott and Morpeth:

Bedlington to North Seaton and Newbiggin:

Newsham to Blyth:

New Bridge Street (Newcastle), through Jesmond, Gosforth, Benton, Backworth (connection to Earsdon Junction), Whitley and Cullercoats to North Shields Terminus or to North Shields and Tynemouth: Whitley to Hartley via the Avenue Branch and Dairy House Junction.

At the end of the last full year, 1873, the stock list of the Blyth & Tyne showed

37 locomotives and tenders

77 coaches of various kinds

3,155 chaldron waggons

185 goods wagons, covered vans, coke, cattle and timber trucks, brake vans and ballast wagons.

The track route was 43 miles in length though another sixteen miles had been authorised and not built. In addition to the various stations and associated buildings there were the engine sheds and workshops at Percy Main.

The North Eastern Railway itself only came into existence a mere twenty years before the Blyth & Tyne Railway lost its independence. It was formed in 1854 by the amalgamation of the York, Newcastle & Berwick, the York and North Midland Railway and the Leeds Northern Railway, all three being significant companies in their own right. The Stockton & Darlington Railway and the Newcastle &

Carlisle Railway were absorbed into the NER, but these (the world's first public railway and the country's first cross country route) were not the only ones by any means. In twenty years their system contained no less than 53 formerly independent public companies and 21 private companies or individuals, all gradually brought together by mergers and take overs. Another eight lines were constructed jointly with other companies.

The territory of the North Eastern Railway included the trunk line north from Doncaster to Berwick; and the area from Leeds to Hull, Tebay and Penrith to Middlesbrough and from Carlisle to Sunderland. It virtually held a monopoly in the north east of England and owned among other things extensive land, canals, docks, hotels, gas works and quarries.

Against such a formidable display of power and influence it would be understandable if one assumed that the Blyth & Tyne Branch would be quietly lopped off and left to rot - but far from it. The Company realised what an important asset it had acquired and considerable sums of money were invested which the Branch repaid with interest. So what developments did take place over the ensuing years?

It will be recalled that the Blyth & Tyne terminus at Morpeth was alongside the North Eastern's main line station but Blyth & Tyne Branch trains continued to use it until May 1880 when they were transferred to a bay platform on the main station. The former goods shed and coal cells were used for another hundred years. In 1882 a curve was authorised from north of Morpeth station to join the Branch between Morpeth and Hepscott. This would have saved reversals at the main station but for some reason it was not put in until 1980.

In June 1872 an Act of Parliament had given the Blyth & Tyne Railway permission to change its route between Whitley Station and Tynemouth, to take the line nearer the coast. It also authorised the Company to abandon the original line when the new one was built. No progress was made, however, and the proposal lay dormant when the NER take-over was completed. A revised scheme was laid before Parliament almost immediately and an Act was passed on 29 June 1875. This approved the new coastal route but a change at the Tynemouth end enabled the line to swing round and join up with the North Eastern's existing Newcastle to Tynemouth route via Wallsend. To achieve this meant lifting the tracks into the former Blyth & Tyne terminus which, being then totally isolated, was no longer used.

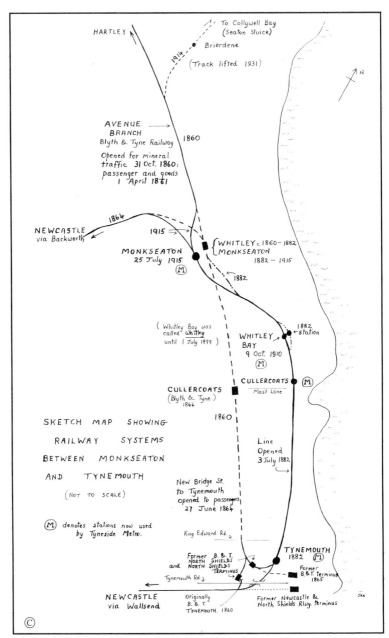

Fig. 2

A very impressive new station for Tynemouth was designed by William Bell who, in 1877, had been appointed Chief Architect for the North Eastern Railway and who held the post until he retired in 1914, after serving the company for 57 years. This majestic building, large and spacious, with an extensive hipped, glass roof was built to reflect its projected importance as a station for handling thousands of commuters, holiday-makers and day-trippers. Other stations were at Monkseaton, Whitley and Cullercoats. (Monkseaton was actually the former *Whitley* station of the Blyth & Tyne Railway.) The new line was opened on 3 July 1882 and, with the exception of some sidings at Monkseaton and Tynemouth, the old route was abandoned. The new Whitley was renamed Whitley Bay on 1 July 1899, then in 1910 a new small but imposing station was built on realigned track there, alongside the existing one, again to the design of William Bell. It was brought into use in October. Major re-positioning of track at Monkseaton some years later meant a replacement station was required. This was opened on 25 July 1915, during World War I. With its uncluttered appearance there were similarities in its design with those at Tynemouth and Whitley Bay. The redundant sections of track from Newcastle via Backworth and from Hartley were removed and the old Blyth & Tyne station was demolished. Part of Sowter Park now covers the site.

The provision of much improved shipping facilities for coal at Blyth is discussed in the next chapter but in 1886 the Ashington Colliery complex was joined to the NER system at Hirst station, which was opened in 1878 and renamed Ashington in October 1889. It meant that coal from that district no longer had to be taken on to the main line north of Morpeth and be conveyed via Bedlington and Newsham. The route from Newsham to shipping staiths at South Blyth was becoming so congested that a new line, one and a half miles in length, was laid from Newsham to coincide with the opening of the New Blyth staiths in May 1888. To the south of North Seaton station a line was opened in 1896 from Marcheys House Junction so that traffic could be taken direct to North Blyth (see page 18).

The NER sought permission in 1894 to build a railway between Blyth and Cramlington but opposition from Lord Hastings, who feared losing the wayleaves he enjoyed from existing routes, led to the Bill being withdrawn.

Blyth's first station was opened in 1847 near the shipyard. A larger station to the west, opened in 1867, was rebuilt between 1894 and

1896 by the local firm of J & W Simpson for £20,000. Two brothers, John and William, established the business in the early 1870s: today it is managed by Brian Simpson, great-grandson of John. Railway contracts have included the following:-

1889-90	houses at South Newsham	(£2,825)
1890-92	the fine station buildings at Morpeth	(£6,975)
1896	Station Master's house at Seghill	(£323)
1899	Jesmond Station	(£5,254)
1903-04	Heaton Electric Car Sheds	(£1,561)

(Note: The Company does not hold plans of these projects.)

It was about this time that Sir George S Gibb, General Manager of the NER, became strongly in favour of making practical use of the company's statistics. He sought to impress on his officials how the work done in carrying passengers and merchandise could be measured against the costs involved so that period could be compared with period, district against district. In 1900 he was able to produce the results of numerous calculations to show, for example, that "the average train load of merchandise and live stock was 44.18 tons and of minerals 92.49 tons (including the mileage of returning empty wagons); the average haul of goods and minerals was 22.23

One of the features of Tynemouth station was the attractive display of shrubs and flowers in a profusion of tubs and hanging baskets. It must have made travellers feel very welcome. (Author's collection)

miles; the average rate per ton/mile for mineral traffic was .99d and for goods traffic 1.642d . . . the average number of passengers per train was only 62.10, and the distance travelled by them was 13.87 miles . . ." (W W Tomlinson: *The North Eastern Railway - Its Rise & Development.)* It is interesting to note that the Blyth & Tyne Railway used to engage in similar cost-cutting exercises throughout its existence. In the light of these calculations, management of the North Eastern Railway introduced new methods of working and a complete re-organisation of the system.

It had not gone unnoticed that there had been a considerable loss of revenue when electric trams were introduced on Tyneside in 1902. In a six month period there was a reduction of 18,000 first class and four million third class passengers on the system as a whole, compared with 1901. A decision was taken, therefore, to electrify the lines between New Bridge Street and Newcastle Central via Tynemouth. This was completed in stages during 1904 (see Chapter 5, page 48, et seq.). At the same time the Company electrified a section of the main line between Heaton and Benton Quarry and laid in the Benton south east curve to join the line to Tynemouth at Benton East signal box. The south west curve provided a connection between Benton Quarry and Benton station in the opposite direction. A north west curve was also approved but not built, though a 1904 picture post-card depicting an electric train in the Up platform at Benton station, with the destination blind showing New Bridge Street, clearly shows three pairs of signals at the end of the Down platform. Those for the proposed north west curve had wooden crosses fastened over them to show they were not in use. Obviously, one set of signals, home and distant, would be removed when it was decided not to proceed with that connection.

In January 1909 a link was created between Jesmond and the main line at Manors, a satellite station of Newcastle. Thereafter passenger trains were withdrawn from New Bridge Street terminus and used Manors North instead. The former Blyth & Tyne area then became a goods yard handling mainly coal for city merchants.

With the prospect that Seaton Sluice could be developed into a small town, the North Eastern Railway Company considered the possibility of extending the electrified area a little further along the coast to a proposed terminus off the Avenue branch which would be called Collywell Bay, and with an intermediate station (convenient for St Mary's Island) to be named Brierdene. In July 1912 a letter was

sent to Seaton Delaval Council requesting permission to divert a
footpath and construct a subway at Brierdene Station. This was
granted. The following October a letter from the Railway Company
enquired whether the Council would favour changing the name of
Seaton Sluice village to Collywell Bay. The Clerk was instructed to
reply that while the Council had no objections to the names chosen
for the stations they would not consider altering the name of Seaton
Sluice. Platforms were built and rails were laid but they were never
used for traffic as the outbreak of war prevented the project from
being completed. An armoured train with a rail-mounted naval gun
for coastal defence was based on the line for a time and older
residents recall empty coal wagons being stored there during the
miners' strike of 1921. In that year councillors complained that bus
fares were exorbitant and insisted a railway link was a necessity. A
deputation was sent by the Council to discuss matters with railway
officials but the Company pointed out that the building of houses had
not materialised and the expense of providing a train service could
not be justified. The track was subsequently taken up in 1931 and
only an embankment and bridge abutments remind us of what might
have been.

   North Eastern Railway stations varied enormously in size, shape and
construction, depending largely on their original purpose. Some
were of stone, others of brick, many were built partly of wood and
glass - yet there was a distinctive 'NER-ness' about them. A typical
smaller station would have a booking office, waiting room, possibly
a ladies room, also a house for the Station Master either on the
platform or situated nearby. The booking office would have tickets
in racks with spare ones in special drawers or cupboards, a ticket-
dating machine, a cash drawer with wooden cash bowls, an
assortment of luggage labels, a weighing machine and the inevitable
glue pot and brush for sticking labels and stamps on to parcels and
luggage. The waiting room with its wooden bench seats would have
a coal fire in cold weather - even a bucket of coal standing in the
hearth - and a cast iron fender. Oil lamps were replaced only
gradually by gas though oil was used at some stations even in the
1970s. Outside there would be luggage, parcels and milk churns on
the platform; sometimes open boxes of soft fruits, even a calf in a sack
waiting to be conveyed by passenger train, its legs tied in a sitting
position and with only its head and shoulders protruding. There were
hanging fire buckets filled with water or sand, posters on notice

boards and enamel advertisements for Bovril, tea, soap, grate polish, cigarettes (Woodbines?) . . . The name of the station and that on the front of the signal box were also in enamel in chocolate and cream colours, so were the smaller notices stating *Porters, Waiting Room, Private,* etc. Company initials abounded. They were on uniform buttons, hats, lapels, ink wells, pen nibs, lamps, oil vessels and even in tiny letters on roofing tacks! In the goods yard there would be an assortment of 'foreign' wagons (i.e. from other companies) lettered LY for Lancashire and Yorkshire, MR (Midland Railway), GN (Great Northern) or GC for Great Central - to name but a few. The rest would be the NER's own stock. Signals on wooden posts were lower quadrant types - that means they pointed down at an angle of about 45 degrees when in the clear-to-proceed position. To the casual observer locomotives were green and passenger coaches crimson lake. They were lettered North Eastern, or North Eastern Railway.

After the take over of the Blyth & Tyne Railway the North Eastern would want to mask the identity of that Company as far as possible. Locos would be repainted in NE colours and lined out but various North Eastern types would be seen almost immediately on Blyth & Tyne metals. Conversely, former B&T engines would range much further from home or be transferred altogether. Passenger coaches in mahogany livery would continue to be used if still in reasonable condition but over the ensuing months would be repainted in standard NE colours. They, too, would be used as required over the system and traditional vehicles of the new Company would replace them or complement those remaining. In the early days, coaches of the North British Railway, which the Blyth & Tyne used to borrow when necessary under traffic agreements, would not be in evidence as it was still a rival company. It is possible the bulk of the chaldron waggons would remain in the area and it would be several years before all former ownership markings were removed. In 1901 the NER still owned 1,862 of these vehicles but they were quickly phased out as more modern stock replaced them. Many were sold to collieries for internal use and, significantly, were still conspicuous at some until the 1960s.

The contribution made by the North Eastern Railway to the social and economic development of the area cannot be over emphasised but from January 1923 120 railway companies in Great Britain become grouped, or amalgamated, into four major companies, namely the London & North Eastern Railway; the London, Midland

A view of the old station at Monkseaton which was replaced in 1915. The live rails here have protective wooden sides. (M. Charlton collection).

& Scottish Railway; the Great Western Railway and the Southern Railway. The North Eastern became part of the LNER, which continued for twenty five years until the railways were nationalised on 1 January 1948 and became British Railways. The Blyth & Tyne Branch was in the North Eastern Region, administered from Newcastle. Having inherited a well organised area from the NER, the LNER continued to make full use of the various routes and amenities. This was carried on by British Railways until collieries were closed down when coal production was no longer a viable proposition. In 1940 the north west curve at Benton was finally laid as a diversionary route to and from Newcastle, thus by-passing the vulnerable marshalling yard and engine sheds at Heaton, very much at risk from enemy action, as were viaducts a short distance away.

The three eras in the Branch's history have all reflected reorganisation, new methods, modernisation, improved designs and increased technology, each one building on the foundation of the other yet taking part of it along. Changes and progress are inevitable to meet current demands and good examples of these can be seen at Morpeth. The station buildings, made of stone, are quite distinctive in appearance. The entrance was 'guarded' by two stone lions, which for many years graced the station gardens at Tynemouth, but these were stolen in the autumn of 1989. The booking office and parcels area was, until July 1989, a wooden building standing at right angles to the main structure. There is a hip roof over part of the Up platform (the Up line is usually the one leading towards London) but a similar one on the Down side was demolished after being damaged in the rail accident of May 1969. There are the two through platforms plus the fenced off remains of a third one which was used by trains to and from central Northumberland. A bay platform on the Up side stood opposite a long cattle dock which used to handle heavy livestock traffic bought or sold at the auction mart opposite the station. The track and dock were removed in 1978 to make way for a car park for people wishing to leave their cars at the station and travel on by train. The market itself was flattened some years later. The bay was for trains using the Blyth & Tyne Branch, as previously mentioned.

Around the station, even at the end of 1989, are several reminders of pre-grouping days and of the LNER. There are for example an ancient wrought iron gate at one end of the subway, several typical, large flower pots, a fine example of an NER tile map dating from about 1912, a letter box bearing the initials "VR" (Victoria Regina) and the remains of a drinking fountain. There are also two LNER luggage barrows probably over fifty years old, now in regular use for Red Star Parcels traffic. An old seat, though not with the traditional snake-pattern supports, was scrapped at the same time as the booking office.

Being a junction and a terminus for two branch lines, Morpeth needed quite a lot of sidings and storage areas but some of these were taken up when no longer needed. The line from central Northumberland's Wansbeck Valley into what was platform 3 is now a siding, sometimes used to stable ballast trains. Photographic evidence shows a small turntable but that too has disappeared.

The main yard on the Blyth & Tyne side of the station, which has handled a variety of traffic over the years, was thinned out to enable block loads of pipes for a mammoth natural gas project to be unloaded more easily. Later, part of the yard was used as a depot in connection with the electrification programme. One outstanding feature at the station end of the goods yard is the original terminus building and goods shed of the Blyth & Tyne Railway, now used by private firms. Beyond, the coal cells have only recently been taken out of use.

The new power signal box, opened in October 1978, replaced a very high-standing cabin with traditional levers. Between the north end of the station and the old 'box an ancient four-wheeled coach body stood for many years, used by permanent-way staff. At least two North Eastern Railway trespass notices from the Wilkinson era (1871-1903) survive in good order.

Chapter 3

The Coal Trade

FROM 1874 BLYTH was declining as a coal-shipping port. Only small sized ships could be loaded inside the harbour; even those risked grounding as the weight of coal pressed them further into the water. Some ships had to finish loading outside the harbour, from keels, but this could be a hazardous business and in bad weather they had to run for the Tyne and make up their cargoes from there. Over the years numerous colliers, and other vessels, were sunk or ran aground along the north-east coast.

In 1877 an engineer's report sent to the Chairman of Blyth Harbour Company starkly stated that "Blyth is now at a crisis in its history and unless a move is made forward it must inevitably go back . . . When an improvement takes place in the general trade of the country, Blyth, instead of sharing in it, will be left out in the cold". Four years later work was put in hand to remove silt and to deepen the channel of Blyth harbour. The following year (1882) a Board of Commissioners under the chairmanship of Sir Matthew White Ridley, Bart., MP (whose family owned much of the land in the area) was formed with the object of taking over the management of the harbour and the development of the port. In that year only 93 ships visited Blyth and coal shipments from both sides of the river were less than 157,000 tons. Horses were still used to haul wagons to and from the spouts on the existing staiths, some of which had belonged to the early days of the Blyth & Tyne Railway Company.

During 1880 the Harbour Company had arranged with the North Eastern Railway for the construction of two coaling staiths and a deep water quay at the south side of the river which would displace some old structures. When J Watt Sandeman was appointed engineer in 1883 he reported that there were two coaling staiths on the north side having a depth of about nine feet at low water. On the south side four small staiths were dry at low water but two others with a depth of about fifteen feet were nearly completed. They were erected by the NER on the Low Quay at a cost of £25,000, were 1,100 feet in length and more than twice the height of the old ones. There were four spouts arranged in pairs , 87½ feet apart. From the reception sidings, loaded wagons were pushed up the incline by locomotives, the coal was tipped through the bottom doors and the empty wagons ran back to the sidings by gravity. The staiths, which were brought into use on 28 February 1884, could accommodate two steamers, each 350 feet long, for loading simultaneously. Coal was tipped from the wagons by *teemers* and levelled in the ships by *trimmers*. Shipments from the south side of the river in that year rose rapidly to 252,780 tons compared with 42,176 tons the previous year. W W Tomlinson's figures *(The North Eastern Railway, Its Rise & Development)* for 1886 were 429,961 tons and in the following year 466,983 tons despite a seventeen week miners' strike. Because of the demand the NER opened another range of staiths (New Blyth) to the east of Low Quay in May 1888, 1,237 feet in length and with four spouts. These and the reception loops could be reached either from South Blyth or via the new line from Newsham.

The construction of staiths was always preceeded by numerous letters, meetings, discussions, arguments and compromises between the various parties - railway, collieries and harbour - each one trying to protect its own interests and blaming the others for intransigence! Such was the case between the NER, Blyth Harbour Commission and the owners of Ashington, Cowpen and Bedlington collieries when improved shipping facilities were sought on the north side of the River Blyth. In one of the Bills promoted by the North Eastern Railway in the 1893 session of Parliament, powers were sought to construct staiths at North Blyth and to double and extend the Cambois branch. Coal shipments from the south side by then were exceeding two million tons a year. The North Blyth staiths were erected and in use by July 1896 though initial discussions had started in 1885. They provided four new berths with two spouts each which greatly facilitated the despatch of coal from collieries around Ashington and Newbiggin. Trains could reach North Blyth via Marcheys House Junction or from Bedlington through West Sleekburn Junction. Thereafter, it was customary for many coal trains from the Morpeth branch to reverse at Bedlington. If the *set* had only one brake van this had to be shunted on to the other end of the train before it could leave Bedlington: one at each end saved a lot of time.

Improvements at Blyth harbour had included east and west break-waters, the widening and deepening of the entrance channel to the port, turning space for ships, the removal of a ridge of rock and better facilities for cargo ships. Nevertheless, it was decided to construct a fourth set of staiths at the west end of the harbour. These were

40-ton and 20-ton coal wagons at Ashington Colliery. (R Miles collection)

completed in 1928, in LNER days, and ran in a north-south direction.
They could accommodate two ships at a time, each 500 feet long, and
were equipped with two belt conveyors plus one gravity spout. Even
the largest vessels could be loaded at any state of the tide. Shipments
continued to grow until, in 1961, Blyth became Europe's busiest coal-
handling port when 6,889,317 tons were despatched. By then not
more than forty hours elapsed from the time a ship was ready to load
until she sailed. Any surge in demand for power, in London for
example, was felt in the small port of Blyth three days later.

On the Tyne, too, vast quantities of coal were carried every day but
in order to appreciate what the railways did nationally and make
some sense out of figures it is worth quoting from *Our Iron Roads* by
F S Williams, a book published in 1883:-

"During the year 1881 the weight of minerals carried was 174,000,000
tons on the railways of the United Kingdom. If the average load is
estimated at, say, seven tons a truck, the minerals conveyed would
fill more than 24,000,000 trucks; and, as the ordinary length of a truck
is about five yards, these wagons would every day form a train 190
miles long, reaching from London as far as York, and in the course
of a year these trucks would stretch from one end to another of a
railway 68,000 miles long, or nearly three times round the world."

His calculations may be very general but the ideas behind them are
thought-provoking.

In 1901, 90% of the NER's mineral wagons were of 8 or 10 tons
capacity: the other 10% included chaldron waggons which carried
just over 2½ tons. Obviously, the lower the capacity the more wagons
were need to move a given load. Furthermore the weight of each
wagon (the tare) *and* the load together had to be considered, then
there was the question of maintenance. As far back as May 1865
Edward Fletcher (Locomotive Superintendent) had given a paper to
the Institute of Civil Engineers on the maintenance of railway rolling
stock. He stated that a single 8-ton coal wagon which cost £90 in 1864
had an annual maintenance cost of £5 10s 0d. Three chaldron
waggons to carry the same amount would have cost £75 but needed
£13 a year spent on them. Over a five year period, the total cost for
an eight-tonner would be £117 10s 0d and for three chaldron
waggons £140. The first experiments made by the Company with
wagons of higher capacity were with those carrying loads of 15 and
32 tons. The tare of the former was 7 tons 16 cwts. and of the latter
13 tons. Twenty fully-loaded 15 tonners, for example, would give a

train weight of 456 tons, whereas *ten* 32-tonners would have a gross weight of 450 tons.

Wagons of 20 tons capacity were introduced by the North Eastern Railway in 1902 and built as the standard hopper coal wagon in huge numbers. They first appeared in May of that year from Shildon Works to a carefully thought out, robust, design, with eight bottom doors for rapid unloading. Timber was used for the bodies which were fastened to the underframes by forged stanchions, corner plates and timber stanchions on the ends. Most had brake handles on the side though some were fitted on the end of wagons. The tare weight was about 9 tons. Train loads of these wagons were a regular feature on the Blyth & Tyne Branch for years, particularly as the design was continued by the LNER. Many were scrapped after twenty-five years of service but at the end of 1941 12,843 of the NER wagons remained. At the end of 1948 2,796 were still in use on the LNER and some were running in the late 1950s. Numerous collieries bought up redundant vehicles and these could be seen well into the 1980s. This type of wagon was the forerunner of the 21-ton all steel mineral truck.

The North Eastern, always a progressive Company, also introduced 40-ton mineral wagons which were carried on two four-wheeled bogies. These appeared in 1903 and were forty feet in length over the buffers, eight feet wide and ten feet in height. They were of all steel construction. One hundred were built for working only between the Ashington collieries and Blyth, hence they were unique to part of the Blyth & Tyne Branch. These wagons were fitted with automatic brakes operated from the engine but reports indicate this system was not always used. In 1923 the LNER purchased thirty similar wagons from the Leeds Forge Company which were also to be used exclusively between Ashington and Blyth. 40-ton wagons were phased out until there were only seventeen left at the end of 1943. A newspaper report of a derailment at North Blyth staiths (see page 131) in 1950, however, showed one of the wagons involved was a 42-ton truck made from steel. Part of at least two of these vehicles remained in internal use at Ashington in the early fifties by permanent way staff. They seem to have been used as flat wagons.

It is worth reflecting on the tremendous amount of organisation needed to ensure the turn round of wagons. Collieries provided coal not only for transfer by ship but for factories, gas works, industrial and domestic use over a wide area. They required a daily supply of empty wagons of various tonnages which were sorted, loaded, made up into sets then placed ready for collection by the railway company. Where did all the wagons come from? What happened if a ship had been delayed and full train loads were waiting to be discharged? What would be done when there were too many wagons for one particular train but not enough for another? Would there be sufficient engines of the right power, or crews for the trains? How would the traffic get through if there had been a derailment? These were some of the problems faced by Mineral Control at Newcastle which could only be solved by co-operation between the staith-master, the collieries and various departments of the railway.

In July 1937 the LNER and the LMS companies agreed new routes for coal traffic. Copies of the book of routes were sent to all collieries with a request that traffic should be consigned and labelled accordingly.

During World War II the demand for coal increased dramatically. Ships were in short supply therefore much more coal had to be moved by rail to the south and midlands. Enemy action frequently caused damage, delays and diversions yet coal movement was only one of the problems the railways had to face - there was also the transportation of food, munitions, and making vital contributions to the movement of service personnel and their equipment. Numerous collieries throughout the country had fleets of their own colourful coal wagons mainly of 10 or 12 tons capacity. During the war wagons constructed to railway standards were permitted to be used throughout the railway system in order to cut down on empty running when returning to their bases. Known to railwaymen as POWS (privately owned wagons) they were frequently seen in rakes of fifty on the Blyth & Tyne Branch. Though their colours had often faded they presented an attractive variation to the mundane grey of railway company coal wagons, as they bowed and nodded to one another over the rail joints. The usual brake van at the end of these loose-coupled trains was the standard 20-ton 16ft. wheelbase type with platform ends. The shorter ten- or twenty-tonners were seen less often but from time to time unusual ones appeared on the branch including six-wheelers, an eight-wheeled former Great Northern Railway one, an old Midland Railway type with a narrow platform at one end and a Cheshire Lines variety bearing large CL letters.

Variety of a different kind was provided between Seaton Delaval and Seghill South cabin in that colliery trains had running rights over the railway company's lines. That stretch of track, or part of it, had originally formed a section of the Blyth & Tyne Railway and from 1874 the Seaton Delaval Coal Company continued to make use of this line. From Seghill, their trains travelled on the Cramlington Coal Company's line to Percy Main. These two companies amalgamated in 1929 to form the Hartley Main Collieries. At that time they had twenty-eight engines between them, with sheds and workshops at Seaton Delaval. Their trains were hauled by a variety of tender and tank locomotives dismissed from service with the North Eastern or from other lines throughout the country. On a Saturday afternoon several of their locomotives travelled in ones and twos from Cramlington and Seghill for maintenance. Each one had to be examined and passed regularly by railway officials before it could travel on railway company lines. Engines working over this stretch included the following:-

No. 3   a former NER outside-framed 0-6-0 built in 1867 which worked until 1959.

No. 6   an 0-6-0 built by Robert Stephenson & Co. in 1899; scrapped in 1960.

No. 8   a Seaton Delaval Coal Co. engine, this 0-6-2 tank was built by Hawthorn Leslie in 1920; scrapped in 1965.

No. 9   another Hawthorn Leslie product from 1921. This was an 0-6-0 tank with outside cylinders, formerly Cramlington Coal Co number 3. Scrapped in 1968 at Harrington, Cumberland.

No. 20   built by Dübs of Glasgow for the Great Northern Railway in 1882. Worked until 1946. This loco had a domeless boiler until 1930.

No. 21   0-6-0 saddle tank named "Skiddaw Lodge". Built by Hudswell Clark, Leeds, this was LMS no. 11568, originally from the Cleator & Workington Junction Railway as number 10.

No. 25   built by the North British Locomotive Co. in 1905 for the Barry Railway, number 132, this 0-6-0 saddle tank became GWR number 747. It was scrapped in 1933 and bought by Hartley Main Collieries.

During 1957 an experimental Gyro engine worked at Seaton Delaval. It was charged from an electrical contact arm and worked on a fly-wheel principle.

(Information supplied by Mr Tom Allan)

The wagons they used had also seen good service on railway company tracks. They had their own brake vans too but for several years up to 1952 a cross between a brake van and a stage coach stood rusting in a siding. It appears that it was used at one time as the wages coach. Seaton Delaval colliery closed in 1960 but the workshops continued to carry out repairs until 1964.

Steel-bodied 16-ton mineral wagons were produced in large numbers by the LNER and the LMS from 1945, at the end of the war, to supplement the stock which had suffered from lack of maintenance for years. In 1961 there were still 25 collieries sending coal for shipment at Blyth, most of which were within a radius of seven miles. The railways, however, were by then looking towards more efficient handling and were favouring block loads in merry-go-round trains.

In the October 1963 issue of *Transport Age,* a magazine then published by the British Railways Board, an article, "New Ways With Bulk", outlined the way ahead. Three quarters of the national output of coal was carried by rail and already 39% of that was being hauled in full train loads but "loading and unloading in trainload bulk could save up to 90% of wagons used and eliminate marshalling." Railways were no longer thinking about carrying consignments of five million tons in egg-cups of 20 tons! An example was quoted of the typical rail layout of a colliery, modernised since the war, covering some 250 acres, "a fine, animated scene of British Railways locomotives shunting empty wagons and loaded wagons and brake vans; of National Coal Board locomotives going to and fro from the empty sidings to the screens and reshuffling them from the screens to the loaded sidings or to the storage sidings." By contrast, a layout for merry-go-round (i.e. continuously-coupled trains in circuit) would require only four acres where "the train complete, indivisible, runs under the bunker, draws up three times as each rake of wagons is loaded, and departs." It envisaged that when the system was in full operation work which at present required 200,000 wagons could be done by 10,000.

Prior to the introduction of merry-go-round trains between collieries and power stations, test trains were arranged in July 1967 on the Blyth & Tyne Branch. Two Type 1 (1,000 h.p.) diesel locos in multiple left Gateshead depot at 9.25 a.m. and proceeded to Newcastle Central Yard to attach two 'fitted' brake vans. They proceeded to Lynemouth Colliery to pick up thirty 24½ ton loaded hopper wagons. Fifteen of these were detached at Newsham and the train continued with a gross load of 550 tons to Percy Main North, where the locos ran round. The train was next taken to Rising Sun Exchange, then back to Percy Main,

An old workhorse of the North Eastern Railway, Seaton Delaval Coal Co., Hartley Main Collieries and the National Coal Board, 'Number 3' was regularly seen on the Blyth & Tyne line between Seaton Delaval and Seghill hauling colliery trains. It was built in 1867 by Robert Stephenson & Co. (NER class number 658) and scrapped in 1959.

LNER Q5 number 644 reversing past the spiral cleaning plant at Ellington colliery in the 1920s. (R Miles collection)

from there past Holywell and along to Burradon Exchange sidings. Returning to Holywell, one loco was uncoupled and ran round the train, which afterwards proceeded to Blyth power station. The second loco followed the train to Blyth and the two took it back to Newsham where it was joined again with the fifteen wagons left there. When all was prepared for the next test run to Widdrington on the main line, the diesels returned light to Gateshead. The crews for these runs were provided by Cambois Depot, opened in 1968 to replace the sheds at North and South Blyth.

In 1968 collieries supplying coal in 24½-ton wagons to Blyth power station were:-

Collieries	Trains per week	Tonnage
Backworth	10	6,500
Rising Sun	12	7,800
Weetslade	5	3,250
Bates	5	3,250
Ashington	21	13,650
Linton	13	8,450
Ellington	18	11,700
Lynemouth	11	7,150
Widdrington opencast	17	11,050
Linton opencast	7	4,550
Dudley	3	1,950
	122	79,300

18 train crews were scheduled to work these services.

Since that time only one colliery remains but coal continues to be brought to Blyth power station from a wider area.

This chapter has shown how the handling of coal has changed from rumbling along in chaldron waggons to complete merry-go-round trains and how the railway companies who owned the Blyth & Tyne Branch have consistently played an indispensable part in carrying what was the life-blood of the nation. Sadly as the coal ran out or became too expensive to mine, pits closed and with them went much of the railway system which served them.

DESCRIPTION OF WAGONS USED AT ASHINGTON COLLIERIES (circa 1923)

SIZE Tons	AVERAGE TARE T. C.	AVERAGE CAPACITY T. C.	HEIGHT From Rails ft. ins.	LENGTH BUFFER TO BUFFER ft. ins.	LENGTH INSIDE ft. ins.	WIDTH INSIDE ft. ins.	WIDTH OUTSIDE ft. ins.	REMARKS
10	6 - 0	9 - 10	7 - 4	18 - 11	16 - 1	7 - 11½	8 - 3½	Loco wagon. Side door.
10	6 - 2	9 - 9½ tons	7 - 5½	19 - 4	16 - 6	7 - 9¼	8 - 1½	Tapered body. Bottom board. Width at bottom 7ft. 8ins.
15	7 - 11	15 - 0	8 - 5½	23 - 0	20 - 0	7 - 3¼	7 - 8	Side door wagon used in New Bridge St. traffic.
20	8 - 15	18 - 0	9 - 8	22 - 8¼	20 - 1	8 - 1	8 - 4½	Loco wagon. Side door.
20	8 - 16	19 - 10	9 - 10	22 - 7	20 - 2	7 - 4	7 - 8	Ordinary bottom door.
20	9 - 5	19 - 0	9 - 8	23 - 10	21 - 0	8 - 2	8 - 6	Hopper wagon. Sliding bottom door.
All the wagons above have ordinary lever side brakes.								
32	13 - 10	28 - 10	9 - 2	39 - 2	35 - 0	7 - 10	8 - 2	Wheel at end operates brake.
40	16 - 7	39 - 10	10 - 0½	39 - 10	35 - 0	7 - 5¼	7 - 9½	Wheel at end operates brake.
40	18 - 10	39 - 10	10 - 0½	44 - 7	41 - 8	8 - 0	8 - 4	New 40 tonner. Brakes operated by two levers at each side.
15	7 - 5	14 - 10	8 - 3	22 - 11	19 - 0	7 - 0	7 - 4	Mineral wagon. Bottom board. Ordinary lever side brakes.

[Information taken from carbon copy of typescript.]

Fig. 3

Chapter 4

Passenger Traffic

THE STUDY OF travel on the railways of Great Britain is a fascinating subject but a worthwhile introduction to such a project would be to examine the development of passenger carriages on the North Eastern Railway, as it was always in the vanguard of progress.

In the early 1870's most of the coaches on the NER were still of the short, four wheeled type though improved in comfort and seating capacity over the years. Older first class carriages were reclassified as second or third class when new designs appeared. Longer third class carriages with six compartments, constructed between 1869 and 1871, gave more space to passengers, especially between the seats, but still retained the low partitions which separated the compartments. Under the Regulations of Railways Act of 1868 railway companies had to provide smoking areas on every train containing more than one carriage of each class unless exempted by the Board of Trade - but a carriage had been fitted up as a smoking saloon for first class passengers on the Tynemouth branch as far back as 1856.

Six wheeled coaches on the North Eastern were introduced in 1872 and quickly built up into an extensive stock. They were used at first on express trains but many were later transferred to branch lines or used mainly for excursion traffic. The NER ceased building them in 1897.

The Company started to produce large numbers of bogied vehicles in 1896, very robust, attractive-looking coaches with a clerestory roof and separate compartments. Most of these were 52 feet in length though a few were 45 feet and there were numerous variations in detail. The style continued in production for ten years by which time all NER trains in normal service consisted of bogie coaches. Then, between 1899 and 1906, almost 250 low-roof carriages were constructed with an improved internal finish. After that their design of coaches favoured an elliptical roof. Initially all these vehicles were lit by gas carried in cylinders on the underframe. At main stations these were replenished by pipes from a storage tank but at small termini it was usual to draw a supply from a gas cylinder wagon parked in a convenient spot, which had two or three cylindrical tanks running the length of the body. Gas lamps in the coaches were lit by a gas-lighter or lamplighter walking along the roof.

All three types of coach - the clerestory, low-roof vehicles and those with elliptical roofs were used throughout the Blyth & Tyne Branch, some of the first two types lasting until 1951. Main line stock appeared, too, especially on excursions to the coast, but they are beyond the scope of this chapter.

When a passenger train reached its destination one of several things could be done with the locomotive.

It could

take water if needed at the platform after running round its train, then await its next departure;

return to the shed for preparation before its next trip;

hand over the train to another engine;

be employed on shunting duties around the station with luggage vans, carriage trucks, horse boxes, or indeed any other vehicle.

It would all depend on the circumstances. *Running round* the train meant uncoupling the engine, drawing forward over the points, setting back along a separate line, reversing through points at the other end and coupling up again to the train. This could waste time, especially if it had arrived late and schedules were tight. To overcome this the North Eastern Railway introduced the 'autocar' system in 1905 where the locomotive was coupled between coaches and used as a push-and-pull train. The driver sat in a special compartment at the front end of the leading coach, which was provided with circular lookout windows, and at first passed instructions to the fireman on the engine by means of a speaking tube. Sometimes only one coach was used. Later, provided the stock was properly equipped and converted, it was possible for the engine to remain at one end of several coaches all the time, which saved shunting. Motive power for autocars initially were class BTP (bogie tank passenger) 0-4-4 well-tanks until they were replaced by class 0 locos of the same wheel arrangement.

The next step forward was the intensive service of electric trains to and from the coast which has already been mentioned and which is explained in greater detail in the next chapter.

When the Blyth & Tyne Railway opened the line from New Bridge Street to Tynemouth in 1864, passenger traffic between Monkseaton and Hartley via the Avenue Branch was withdrawn except for occasional use. The August 1877 timetable (fig. 4) which cost one old penny, shows a Sunday evening train leaving Morpeth at 9.15 travelling via the Avenue to Tynemouth, arriving 10.05. It left at 10.15 and returned through the Avenue to reach Blyth half-an-hour later. *The Avenue* halt was never re-opened but regular, direct services were restored between Monkseaton and Hartley in June 1904 to link up with the new electric trains. This branch continued in use for another sixty years. It saw many thousands of direct services between Monkseaton and Blyth or Newbiggin and hundreds of excursion trains. During the 1950s the Saturday morning Tynemouth to Glasgow summer train used the line: it was occasionally booked to stop at Bedlington. Although the Avenue Branch was single track, towards the end of its life four signals on separate posts were erected alongside one another about 500 yards south of Avenue Crossing signal box, on the right hand side of the track looking towards Monkseaton. These were used for drivers' eye sight testing. All track was lifted about 1965 and part of this route is now a public right of way.

Where traffic on a branch was light, particularly at off-peak times, the LNER put into service 80 steam driven rail-cars built by Sentinel, almost three quarters of which worked in the North East. Three types were used having two, six or twelve cylinders depending on the gradients in the area. At first they were finished in teak-like livery similar to wooden stock but the second batch was turned out in bright red and cream. Later green and cream was adopted as the standard colour scheme. Some hauled a light-weight trailer but there was one articulated unit, the *Phenomena,* which spent all its life working on the Blyth & Tyne Branch, usually between Blyth, Morpeth and Monkseaton. All were named after stage coaches.

A letter from the Station Master at Newsham to signalmen in Newsham North box in October 1937 stated that authority had been given for steam coaches to haul one fully braked vehicle such as a horse box or parcel van. Attached to the letter was a list of services on which these rail-cars were used:

Blyth to Newsham   am   7.52   8.20, 8.52,
                                pm   2.52,   3.52, 5.45 (Sats. excepted),
                                        7.52

Newsham to Blyth	am	8.05,	8.37 9.03,
	pm	3.03,	4.03, 5.55, (Sats. excepted),
		8.03	
Blyth-Monkseaton	pm	1.25,	4.25, 6.25.
Monkseaton-Blyth	pm	2.19,	5.17, 7.17.

NEWCASTLE AND MORPETH via BACKWORTH. 33

Fares from NEWCASTLE (New Bridge Street.) Single 1st	2nd	Gov	DOWN.		Week Days 1 Gov a.m.	2 Gov a.m.	3 Gov a.m.	4 Gov p.m.	5 Gov p.m.	6	7	8	A Gov a.m.	B Gov p.m.	B Gov p.m		Sundays 1 Gov a.m.	2 Gov a.m.	3 C Gov. p.m.	4 Gov p.m.	5 Gov. p.m.
			Newcastle (New Bridge)	Dep		8 20	11 45	4 15	7 45					4 0	6 0			9 45	2 0	7 45	
0 2	0 1½	0 1	Jesmond	"		8 22	11 47	4 17	7 47					4 2	6 2			9 47	2 2	7 47	
0 5	0 3½	0 2	Gosforth	"		8 28	11 53	4 23	7 53					4 8	6 8			9 53	2 8	7 53	
0 8	0 6	0 4	Benton	"		8 34	11 59	4 29	7 59					4 14	6 14			9 59	2 14	7 59	
1 3	1 0	0 8	Tynemouth	Dep		8 20	11 45	4 15	7 45									9 45	2 15	7 45	10 15
1 3	1 0	0 8	North Shields	"		8 22	11 47	4 17	7 47									9 47	2 17	7 47	10 17
1 3	1 0	0 8	Cullercoats	"		8 26	11 51	4 21	7 51									9 51	2 21	7 51	10 21
1 3	1 0	0 8	Whitley	"		8 30	11 55	4 25	7 55									9 55	2 25	7 55	10 25
1 3	1 0	0 8	Backworth	Arr		8 38	12 3	4 33	8 3									10 3	2 33	8 3	
1 0	0 9	0 6	Backworth for Holywell & Earsden	Dep		8 42	12 7	4 37	8 7					4 22	6 22			10 7	2 37	8 7	
1 6	1 1	0 8½	Seghill	"		8 49	12 14	4 44	8 14					4 29	6 29			10 14	2 44	8 14	
1 7	1 2	0 9½	Seaton Delaval	"		8 53	12 18	4 48	8 18					4 33	6 33			10 18	2 48	8 18	
1 9	1 3	0 11	Hartley	"		8 58	12 23	4 53	8 23					4 38	6 38			10 23	2 53	8 23	10 33
2 0	1 6	1 0½	Newsham	"	7 11	9 4	12 29	4 59	8 29					4 44	6 44		7 41	10 29	2 59	8 29	10 39
			Blyth Branch: Newsham	Dep		9 5	12 30	5 0	8 30						6 45			10 30	3 0	8 30	
2 3	1 8	1 2½	Blyth	Arr		9 10	12 35	5 5	8 35						6 50			10 35	3 5	8 35	10 45
			Blyth	Dep	7 0	8 50	12 15	4 45	8 15						6 30		7 30	10 15	2 45	8 15	
			Newsham	Arr	7 5	8 55	12 20	4 50	8 20						6 35		7 35	10 20	2 50	8 20	
2 3	1 8	1 2½	Bebside	Dep	7 18	9 10	12 35	5 5	8 35					4 50	6 50		7 48	10 35	3 5	8 35	Via Avenue Branch.
2 5	1 9	1 3½	Bedlington	"	7 22	9 14	12 39	5 9	8 39					4 54	6 54		7 52	10 39	3 9	8 39	
			Newbiggin Branch: Bedlington	Dep		9 15	12 40	5 10	†8 40						6 55			10 40	3 10	8 40	
2 9	2 0	1 5½	North Seaton	"		9 20	12 45	5 15	8 45						7 0			10 45	3 15	8 45	
3 6	2 8	1 9	Newbiggin	Arr		9 29	12 54	5 24	8 54						7 9			10 54	3 24	8 54	
			Newbiggin	Dep			12 15	4 45	8 15				8 50		6 10			10 15	2 45	8 15	
			North Seaton	"			12 24	4 54	8 24				8 59		6 19			10 24	2 54	8 24	
			Bedlington	Arr			12 29	4 59	8 29				9 4		6 24			10 29	2 59	8 29	
2 8	2 0	1 4½	Choppington	Dep	7 27	9 19	12 44	5 14	8 44						6 59		7 57	10 44	3 14	8 44	
3 0	2 3	1 7	Hepscott	"	7 34	9 26	12 51	5 21	8 51						7 6		8 4	10 51	3 21	8 51	
3 0	2 3	1 4½	Morpeth	Arr	7 38	9 30	12 55	5 25	8 55						7 10		8 8	10 55	3 25	8 55	
			Alnwick	Arr	9 55	12 10	3 20	6 36	10 30								9 50				
			Berwick	"	11 15	1 30	4 30	7 15									11 10				
			Edinburgh	"		3 30	7 0	8 50													

A—Market train, runs on Wednesdays only. B—Market trains run on Saturdays only. † Leaves Bedlington at 8-45 p.m. on Saturdays.
C—Passengers from Newcastle change at Backworth Junction.

N E R TIMETABLE BETWEEN NEW BRIDGE STREET AND MORPETH VIA BACKWORTH, 1877, (DOWN LINE).

Fig 4a. Part of 1877 timetable - Down line

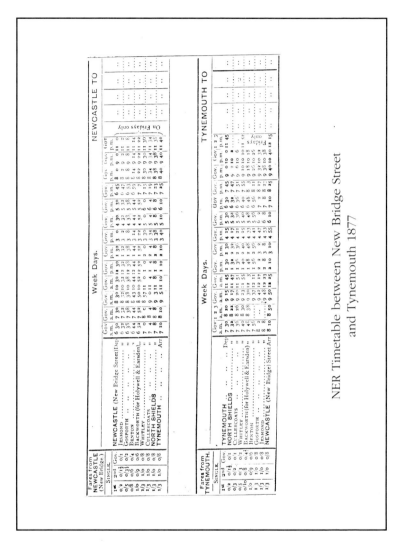

Fig 4b

Entries in the Occurrence Book from that particular cabin relating to steam rail cars make interesting reading. Normally these cars were considered very reliable over the twenty years from 1927 but . . .
"June 18th 1929   The 3.52 pm ex Central Steam Coach
                              "Brilliant" arrived here at 4.39 pm and was

	unable to go forward and had to be shunted to the short end of the Down Independent. Left here again at 5.59 for Central, light, via Backworth.
13th January 1936	The 6.30 pm Ordinary Passenger Blyth to Monkseaton Steam Coach "Phenomena", failed between Blyth and Isabella Box. Assisted to Newsham by Engine No. 1976.
14th March 1943	The 8.43 Ordinary Passenger Steam Coach "Industry" ex Blyth derailed at No. 36 points at 8.50 pm when setting into Branch Platform."

For many years passenger trains ran from New Bridge Street or Manors to Morpeth. A bay platform was provided at Bedlington for connecting trains to Newbiggin. Picture postcards exist showing the large NER sign

BEDLINGTON JUNCTION
PASSENGERS CHANGE FOR NORTH SEATON
ASHINGTON AND NEWBIGGIN

The transfer of traffic from Manors North to Newbiggin meant that passengers had to change at Bedlington for Choppington, Hepscott and Morpeth. Passenger services on this route were withdrawn in 1950.

An analysis of the May - July 1933 LNER timetable between Newcastle, Newbiggin and Morpeth via Backworth reveals the following and will serve as an example:-

FROM MANORS. On weekdays there were trains every hour between Manors North and Newbiggin between 8.24 am and 9.24 pm. Earlier morning departures were at 7.30 and 7.52 am. Only the latter stopped at Jesmond, West Jesmond, South Gosforth and Benton: all others ran non-stop as far as Backworth which was the usual procedure. The 5.24 pm from Manors called at Seghill, Seaton Delaval and Hartley only on Saturdays. The last train left Manors at 10.54 and arrived at Newbiggin 11.53 pm - a total of sixteen plus another one which started from Newcastle.

FROM NEWCASTLE CENTRAL. Apart from the train indicated above which left Central at 1.22 pm there was one departed for Morpeth at

5.35 am which also carried newspapers and mail. It returned to Newcastle via the main line. In addition a train left at 9.56 am, stopped at Manors, then ran express to Blyth in 34 minutes.
FROM BLYTH. One train a day to Newbiggin at 6.44 am and four to Morpeth.
FROM BEDLINGTON. Two trains to Newbiggin, plus one to Morpeth on Saturdays only.
In the Up direction towards Newcastle there were:-
FROM NEWBIGGIN. 15 trains a day to Manors one of which left at 7.37 am and called at every station on the way: 2 to Blyth plus one extra on Saturdays: 2 to Newcastle Central. One left at 8.40 am and stopped at all stations to Newsham. It then ran express apart from stops at South Gosforth, West Jesmond and Manors, an unusual combination.
FROM BLYTH and Newsham to Manors and the Central, 1 express: 1 Saturday night train to Newsham, Hartley and Seaton Delaval only.
FROM MORPETH. 1 as far as Newsham:
              2 to Blyth:
              1 to Bedlington, plus 2 extra on Saturdays.
FROM ASHINGTON. 1 to Blyth except on Saturdays.

The Sunday service was also very reasonable, thus:-
FROM MANORS to Newbiggin 9
FROM BLYTH to Bedlington 1
              to Newbiggin 1
FROM BEDLINGTON to Newbiggin 2
FROM NEWBIGGIN to Manors 9 (the first train also called at Benton)
              to Blyth 2
              to Bedlington 1
FROM MORPETH to Bedlington 1.
   Most trains passing through Newsham had connections to and from Blyth. There were also the electric trains from Newcastle to the coast giving connections at Backworth, and frequent trains between Manors and Newcastle. Relief trains were run to Newbiggin when required.
   Working Timetables were produced for the use of staff but evolving over the years they grew in complexity. They included such information as distances, train make up and classification; departure, passing and arrival times; special working instructions, crew times, speed restrictions and specific notes about each service where

necessary.

The Branch, of course, saw numerous excursion trains from various parts of the country mostly to Whitley Bay and Tynemouth. There were in addition school and Sunday School outings to Newbiggin-by-the-Sea (to give it its full name). Special trains from the Blyth & Tyne were put on for day trips away and to take passengers to destinations for specific purposes such as football matches, agricultural shows, the Miners' Picnic and pantomimes. Sometimes people were conveyed to Morpeth by bus to join the train there. In 1936 trains converged on Sunderland on 1 February for a football match against Chelsea. The cost was 2s 6d (12½p) from Blyth, Bedlington & Bebside; 3s (15p) from Newbiggin and Ashington; 2s (10p) from Newsham and Seaton Delaval. Outings advertised in July 1938 included Rothbury, Edinburgh, Beal for Holy Island, Coldstream and Galashiels. Very popular were the specials which chugged through rural Northumberland to let folk see the station gardens in bloom. The NER set aside 200 guineas annually to be divided among the sixty Best Kept Stations. The stations were divided into four groups each of which were awarded five first class prizes of £6, five second class prizes of £3, and five third class prizes of £1 10s (£1.50) each. No station could take a prize in the same class for more than two years in succession but if deemed worthy it could receive a Special First Class Certificate but no money to share between the staff. For years Tynemouth had beautiful floral displays in tubs, hanging baskets, troughs and pots all over the station. This idea of station gardens was continued by the LNER who provided flower pots and edging for flower beds.

Excursions such as these continued in the British Railways era from the beginning of 1948. A later feature was train loads of railway enthusiasts travelling over the Branch particularly when the train was steam hauled. One such was the Jubilee class loco *Alberta,* number 45562, which headed a special to Ashington Colliery in June 1967. These trains are somewhat rare now but a class 56 diesel took a rail tour train from Plymouth to Morpeth via Bedlington in the autumn of 1987.

In January 1950 the Blyth News reported that British Railways intended to axe a once-daily train from Blyth to Morpeth if no objections were received, thereby ending 90 years of continuous passenger service. At one time the train was well patronised but there were then only two regular passengers. Station staff at Blyth affectionately referred to the train as *The Diners* even though it consisted of

North Eastern Railway.

League Football Match at Newcastle

NEWCASTLE UNITED V. SUNDERLAND

On Saturday, 9th October, 1920,

ADDITIONAL TRAINS

Conveying Passengers at Ordinary Fares, will be run as shewn below.

	a.m.
ASHINGTON ....dep.	11 10
North Seaton .... ,,	11 14
Bedlington .... ,,	11 20
Bebside .... ,,	11 24
Newsham .... ,,	11 30
Hartley .... ,,	11 35
Seaton Delaval ...... ,,	11 39
Seghill .... ,,	11 44
Backworth .... ,,	11 50
Benton .... ,,	11 57
	p.m.
South Gosforth .... ,,	12 2
West Jesmond .... ,,	12 6
Jesmond .... ,,	12 10
MANORS NORTH ...arr.	12 14

For further information apply to District Passenger Manager, Newcastle
Tel. No. 741.

This train is advertised and arranged by the Company subject to the
General Conditions and Regulations specified in the current Time Tables, to
which intending passengers are referred

H.N. 223—Howe Brothers, Printers, Melbourne Street, Gateshead.

Fig 5

three or four suburban coaches - but no dining car, ever!

In British Railways days the old push-and-pull trains with the ex NER class 0 engines (LNER and BR class G5) still shuttled to and fro until replaced by diesel multiple unit trains in 1958.

There have always been diversions along the Blyth & Tyne Branch between Morpeth and Benton Quarry when necessary for derailments or track repairs but when this happens today it is the high-speed trains which go through but very cautiously.

So far in this chapter we have considered mainly routine passenger traffic but other categories can be included because of their general interest. In the days of the NER and LNER it was customary to send a Stores Van along the line or attach it to a passenger train. One such vehicle was a bogied van with spoked wheels. As the train stopped at each station the storeman unloaded various supplies for the office, porters' room and signal-boxes. A typical delivery for a small signal box would be as shown in one Occurrence Book:-

"JULY 24th 1896 Received the following stores-

5 gallons of paraffin oil, 2 gallons of Rape oil,

1 gallon of machine oil, 1 sheet of emery paper,

1 packet of whitening, 1 packet of soda, 1 piece of soap and pipe clay, 2 rolls of lamp wick & 3 lamp chimneys & 1 dozen fog signals."

Other vans could travel on a passenger train (not electric) provided they met coaching stock requirements. These included horse boxes and special cattle vans in which an attendant could travel in a special compartment. These vehicles would be detached en route at the station to which they had been consigned. Pigeon traffic travelled in vans with folding shelves wide enough to accommodate the baskets. One of these would be part loaded at each station. When, however, it was an important race with numerous entries several vans were run together in a special train and joined with others at Newcastle Central. Pigeon traffic was a good source of income on the Blyth & Tyne Branch from the early 1930s. There was also parcels traffic.

During both world wars, Army units were stationed at various points in the area, notably around Blyth, Hartford Camp and Seaton Delaval. Use was made of the railway for moving troops and their equipment into and out of the district. In April 1915 a letter was sent from the Yard Master's Office at Blyth staiths to a freight guard of South Blyth depot. It read:-

ENTRAINING OF NORTHUMBRIAN DIVISION
The General Superintendent writes as follows:-

"I should like all the staff concerned to know that the Military Authorities are exceedingly gratified with the way in which the Railway Company's share of the movement was carried out. I also wish to add that in my opinion the compliment is well earned. It was gratifying to see the hearty way in which all our men carried out their share of the work, they were evidently anxious to make the thing a success, and they certainly succeeded.

The Divisional Superintendent also wishes to convey his own appreciation of the splendid efforts made by the out-door staff to load up and dispatch the trains punctually, and to the clerical staff (including Inspector) and Signalmen who were largely responsible for the train arrangements working so satisfactorily, to which I wish to add my appreciation of the efforts of my staff who were engaged on this important work."

In the 1940s quite a number of military specials left from Seaton Delaval carrying personnel from there and Hartford. As a general rule the empty stock ran through the station on the Down line as far as Newsham with the engine (usually a V2) running tender first. The train was then brought back on the Up line ready for the men to embark. Prior to departing it reversed slowly into the siding where it attached wagons and vans that had been previously loaded.

Something which kept staff on their toes was a visit by high-ranking officers of the Company who travelled in a well-appointed six wheeled coach referred to with some awe as *The Glass Carriage*.

A letter from the NER Engineer's and Passenger Superintendent's Office at Newcastle, dated 7 September 1880, was sent to certain stations. It concerned a Directors' & Officers' Special the following day and stated:-

"The above will leave New Bridge for Blyth direct at 8.35 am, thence running empty to North Blyth via Newsham and Cambois Colliery line, where it will wait the arrival of the Directors &c and then return to Newbiggin which place it will leave for Tynemouth about 1.00 pm via Avenue Branch, stopping at Whitley. It will leave Tynemouth for New Bridge about 4.00 pm. The times given are very uncertain and a good look out must therefore be kept for the Special.

Please note and advise all your Staff concerned and *acknowledge receipt by next train certain.*"

A circular from the LNER District Superintendent's Office, New-castle, dated 3 May 1928, which was sent to all stations and signal boxes, gave instructions on the working of Officers' Specials-
    "The following instructions are to be observed in the working of Officers' Specials:-
    1) A booked Officers' Special (or an unbooked one in a case of emergency such as proceeding to the site of an accident, etc) to be considered of equal importance with Express Passenger Trains and take turn with such trains.
    2) An Officers' Special when making intermediate stops must not be allowed to interfere with the ordinary service."
Top of the list of visiting VIPs is Royalty and the Blyth & Tyne area played host to the Royal Train on several occasions. Planning for such an event has to be meticulous in every detail, especially from the point of safety. The amount of work for every department is always enormous, finally brought together in very precise instructions to officers in charge of stations.
    The Royal Train, consisting of two locomotives and eleven coaches was at Ponteland station in Northumberland on 9/10 October 1928. (The Ponteland Branch was reached by triangular junctions from the Blyth & Tyne at South Gosforth). A very detailed plan was drawn to show the exact position of every vehicle and to indicate what precautions had to be taken around the station and with track. The make up of the train for that visit was:-
    The locomotives - which also heated the Train during the night-

First brake	number	10071
Sleeping Saloon	number	10365
Dining Saloon	number	10411
Saloon	number	10506
Sleeping Saloon	number	10321
Saloon	number	10507
Dining Saloon	number	10400
H.M. The King's Saloon		
H.M. The Queen's Saloon		
Sleeping Saloon	number	10342
First brake	number	10070

An Accumulator Van was attached to the rear of the train on arrival to provide power. A screen train, consisting of six 52 ft suburban coaches was placed so that onlookers could not see the Royal Train from nearby cottages. On October 10 H.M. King George V and H.M.

Queen Mary alighted on the Up platform at Jesmond, first to open a
new school then, later, the new Tyne Bridge.

Ponteland station was again used as a base for the Royal Train from
20-23 February 1939 when visits were made to Tyneside, including
Tynemouth, and County Durham. In the early part of World War II
a Royal visit was made to Blyth when the Train was hauled on the
return journey by an A4 class streamlined locomotive named *Golden
Plover*. The Royal Train was stabled overnight in the Avenue Branch
on 28/29 October 1954 with HM Queen Elizabeth II and HRH Prince
Philip on board. On another occasion it remained overnight along the
Ponteland line, having brought The Duke of Edinburgh from
Aberdeen. The following morning, 27 September 1975, it left via
Jesmond for York where The Duke officially opened the National
Railway Museum. It was a short train consisting of power brake 5154,
Saloon 45006, Royal Saloon 798 and brake 5155. The brake coaches
were clerestory-roofed vehicles.

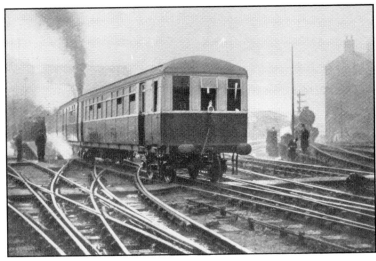

*Steam-powered railcars were introduced by the LNER in 1927 for local
passenger services. An articulated car named 'Phenomena' spent
nearly all its working life on the Blyth & Tyne Branch. This photo-
graph, however, was taken at Kings Cross and the crowd on the
platform suggests an inaugural ceremony. (K. L. Taylor collection)*

Running a railway is a very complicated business most of which is never noticed by the travelling public as so much is done behind the scenes. In some things, nevertheless, passengers are involved when, for example, they forget their belongings as they leave a train. Below are some interesting extracts from the Lost Property Book at Bebside station between 1907 and 1925.

BEBSIDE STATION LOST PROPERTY BOOK 1907 - 1925 (extracts).

DATE	TRAIN FROM	WHERE FOUND OR LEFT	DESCRIPTION	DISPOSAL
19th NOV. 1907	Newsham	Waiting room	Black bag containing bananas	Bedlington
30th OCT. 1908	5.17 Morpeth	By passenger	Brown paper bag containing celery.	Blyth
27th NOV. 1908	6.30 Morpeth	Handed out	Black silk bag containing hankie, ear trumpet.	Forest Hall
17th DEC. 1908	ex Newsham		Packet meat. Destroyed 21st having become putrid.	
7th FEB. 1909	6.30 Morpeth	Handed out	Brown paper parcel containing pair moleskin trousers.	Sent depot
7th AUG. 1909	Up platform		One five shilling piece.	Depot 11/8/09
20th AUG. 1909	ex Backworth		Stool.	F. Gray
24th SEPT. 1909	6.30 Morpeth	3rd Class carriage	Purse 5 x 3½" containing hairpins.	Sent depot
23rd DEC. 1910	Newsham		Gramophone soundbox.	John Reid
22nd JULY 1911	9.30 pm		One pram containing bird-cage, 2 pillows.	Owner
22nd AUG. 1914	Newsham		One brown paper parcel containing couple rabbits.	(Not shown)
1st SEPT. 1914	Morpeth		One straw bag containing 5 handkerchiefs and ball.	Owner
22nd MAY 1915	Bedlington		Parcel leeks.	Sent Backworth
13th AUG. 1920	ex Newsham	3rd Class carriage	Parcel containing rolls of wallpaper.	(Not shown)
22nd AUG. 1922	Morpeth	Handed off train	One bait tin (i.e. food container).	Ashington
25th FEB. 1925		Handed off train	Bag of oranges.	Sold 2nd March

Author's collection

Unfortunately, most records at local level of traffic handled on the branch have been destroyed but those given were extracted from official figures submitted by stations to area offices as fodder for statistics.

BENTON Year ending December 1939
PASSENGER TRAFFIC EXCLUDING SEASON TICKETS
(1st and 3rd CLASS)

	TOTAL	GROSS RECEIPTS		
Standard or ordinary fares	1,403	47	11	8
Day, Half-day and Evening Excursions	83	20	7	3
Special (Experimental) Fares, Day	10,001	200	6	9
Special (Experimental) Fares, Period	63,571	1891	13	6
Cheap day	27	1	15	2
Monthly Return at or above Minimum Fares	69	93	11	6

Workmen	4,922	126 10	5
Privilege	6,294	128 16	5
Bulk Travel	9	7 10	5
Other Reduced Fares	734	63 19	1
Excess Fares	1,213	14 17	9

88,326 £2596 19 11

SEASON & TRADERS TICKETS (1 week, 1 month, 3 months etc.)

	TOTAL	No of Journeys on Annual Basis	RECEIPTS
Tickets at full, half, reduced and privilege rates 1st class	12	3060	77 7 9
3rd class	2596	113798	1558 13 1
Tickets at full, half, reduced privilege rates and traders' tickets (Issued by Passenger Manager or District Passenger Manager) 3rd class	78	7800	56 11 5
	2686	124658	£1692 12 3

PARCEL & OTHER MERCHANDISE TRAFFIC CHARGED AT PASSENGER TRAIN RATES

	Received	Forwarded	Receipts
Parcels under 2cwts	877	791	65 13 6
Cycles, prams, etc. acc passengers	361	718	11 8 6
Excess Luggage			1 7 1
Passengers' Luggage in Advance		104	5 4 6
	1238	1613	£83 13 7

TICKETS COLLECTED 131,674

BEBSIDE PASSENGER TRAFFIC 1961

Passengers booked	14,732
Passenger journeys made	20,086
Parcels forwarded	739
Parcels received	3,838
Paid Luggage in Advance, received	72
forwarded	nil

BLYTH PASSENGER TRAFFIC 1961

Passengers booked	88,918
Passenger journeys made	114,267
Season Tickets issued	98
Parcels forwarded	29,124
Parcels received	33,405
Paid Luggage in Advance, received	386
forwarded	687

NEWSHAM PASSENGER TRAFFIC 1961

Passengers booked	89,041
Passenger journeys made	140,376
Season Tickets issued	42
Parcels forwarded	593
Parcels received	335
Paid Luggage in Advance, received	5
forwarded	67

Each station contributes to the total income of a branch or section of main line, which in turn advances the area and the region, but to stand back and look objectively at the country as a whole and assess the importance of rail travel before the internal combustion engine, one cannot do better than to look again at the graphic details in "Our Iron Roads" as published in 1883.

"We are equally embarrassed by the numbers that tell us of the multitudes of passengers who travel. Instead of the 80,000 persons, who thirty years ago, went by coach 1,500,000 passengers are now carried every day by railway in a fraction of the time and at a fraction of the cost previously required; passengers who would require 70,000 coaches to hold them, and 700,000 horses to draw them. Exclusive of season-ticket holders there were in 1870, 336,000,000 passengers; in 1880, 604,000,000; in 1881, more than 623,000,000 or considerably more than 10,000,000 a week the year through. Now, what do 10,000,000 passengers mean? They mean a number two and half times the population of London. They mean that so many passengers travel that in three weeks the railway passengers are so numerous as the whole population of England and Wales. Ten millions a week means nearly a million and a half a day, who would fill 60,000 first class carriages, which, if each is eight yards long, would make a train which would stretch nearly 300 miles in length, or from London to Newcastle; while the passengers who travelled last year in Great Britain would form a procession 100 abreast a yard apart - extending across Africa from Tripoli to the Cape Colony; or from London across the Channel, France, Switzerland, Italy, the Mediterranean, Egypt, Nubia and Abyssinia to Aden at the southern mouth of the Red Sea, a distance of nearly 3,500 miles; and all this in addition to the journeyings of season-ticket holders, who last year numbered 500,000, many of whom probably travelled 200 or 300 journeys each."

Passenger trains between Bedlington and Morpeth, serving Chop-pington and Hepscott, were withdrawn on 3 April 1950. Newbiggin, Ashington, North Seaton, Bedlington, Bebside, Newsham, Blyth, Hartley, Seaton Delaval and Seghill were closed to passengers on 2 November 1964. Backworth was closed on 13 June 1977.

In spite of this, the platforms at Newsham station were used once a year on three occasions for a special train conveying school children on an end of year outing. In July 1967, for example, staff and pupils from Newlands and Princess Louise County Secondary Schools, Blyth, visited Windermere in the Lake District.

IT'S QUICKER BY RAIL TO LONDON

CHEAP FACILITIES FROM NEWCASTLE

Monthly Return Tickets - daily	47/9
Night Travel Tickets Nightly	35/8
Day Excursions	21/-
Half-day Excursions	15/3

Fig. 6.
Copy of undated cardboard poster found in a station c 1980

DEPARTURE OF TRAINS FROM BLYTH FROM 7 SEPTEMBER 1964
TO CLOSURE OF LINE TO PASSENGER TRAFFIC (2 NOV.1964)

MONDAYS TO FRIDAYS		SATURDAYS	
Time	Destination	Time	Destination
6-08	Monkseaton *		
7-18	Newsham (conn. to Monkseaton)	6-08	Monkseaton *
7-27	Newbiggin	7-18	Newsham (conn. to Monkseaton)
7-50	Newsham (conn. to Manors)	7-27	Newbiggin
8-12	Newsham (conn. to Newbiggin)	7-50	Newsham (conn. to Manors)
8-47	Newsham (conn. to Monkseaton)	8-12	Newsham (conn. to Newbiggin)
9-35	Newsham (conn. to Monkseaton)	8-47	Newsham (Conn. to Monkseaton)
9-55	Manors	9-45	Newsham ***
10-37	Newsham (conn. to Newbiggin)	10-00	Monkseaton
11-00	Monkseaton	10-45	Newsham ***
11-56	Newsham (conn. to Monkseaton)	11-00	Monkseaton
12-35	Newsham (conn. to Newbiggin)	11-45	Newsham ***
13-05	Monkseaton	12-00	Monkseaton
13-56	Newsham (conn. to Monkseaton)	12-45	Newsham ***
14-35	Newsham (conn. to Newbiggin)	13-00	Monkseaton
15-00	Monkseaton	13-45	Newsham ***
15-56	Newbiggin **	14-00	Monkseaton
16-42	Monkseaton	14-45	Newsham ***
17-07	Newsham (conn. to Newbiggin)	15-00	Monkseaton
17-24	Newsham (conn. to Monkseaton)	15-45	Newsham ***
17-44	Newsham (conn. to Newbiggin)	16-00	Monkseaton
18-12	Newsham (conn. to Monkseaton)	16-45	Newsham ***
18-40	Newsham (connections to Newcastle and Newbiggin)	17-00	Monkseaton
		17-44	Newsham ***
19-25	Monkseaton	18-05	Monkseaton
20-00	Newsham (connections to Monkseaton and Newbiggin)	18-45	Newsham ***
		19-00	Monkseaton
20-27	Monkseaton	19-45	Newsham ***
21-23	Newsham (conn. to Manors)	20-00	Monkseaton
22-05	Newsham (conn. to Newbiggin)	20-45	Newsham ***
22-55	Monkseaton	21-00	Monkseaton
23-24	Newsham (conn. to Newbiggin)	21-47	Newsham (conn. to Manors)
		22-19	Newsham (conn. to Newbiggin)
		23-18	Newsham (connections to Newbiggin and Newcastle)
		23-59	Newbiggin

    *   Connection at Newsham for Newbiggin
   **   Connection at Newsham for Monkseaton
  ***   Connections for Newbiggin and Manors
          Trains arriving at Monkseaton connect with electric trains

ANALYSIS ...   ANALYSIS ...
Trains to Manors   1   Trains to Monkseaton   13
          Monkseaton   8   Newsham   19
          Newsham   19   Newbiggin   2
          Newbiggin   2   TOTAL   34
             TOTAL   30

Fig. 7

Mr. Marples turns down "hardship" objections

END OF THE LINE— BUT STILL FIGHTING

A klaxon blares as the last rail journey is made...

Late bid to save Blyth and Tyne service fails

Minister get further protests

EAST Northumberland...
ment that Mr...
the withdrawal...
railway passen...
closure...
But...

HOPE OF REPRIEVE IS SHATTERED BY TRANSPORT CHIEF

By DAVID WILSON

A YEAR of public outcry failed to ... empty seats and at one minu... night on Saturday the last passen... out of the closure of the ... drama of the service.

Driver Tommy Cheesemon, o... klaxon blaring all the way from Bl... a final salute as given by explodi... on the line by railwaymen. Mon... doors of their homes to see the l... its last journey.

Fittingly, the man who whistled Blyth's last diesel away from the station was 70-year-old Mr. Bob Yellowley, whose father helped to lay the line over 75 years ago. Bob was the guard on the first diesel as being the last ...

Bob has worked 52 years on the railway ... and officially re... tired in 1961 but came back again ... and has worked eve... season. But with the closure ... the line he is finally to ret...

Line closes with a bang

MR. BOB YELLOWLY, a 70 - year - old railway guard blew his whistle and brought to an end the 75-year-old history of the Blyth and Tyne passenger line at the weekend

It was appropriate that Mr. Yellowly, of Portland Street, Blyth, was the guard on the 11.59 p.m. train on Saturday from Blyth to Newbiggin, for his father helped to lay the tracks of the line more than 75 years ago.

"I think it is a mistake to withdraw this service," said Mr. Yellowly, who started his retirement yesterday after 52 years on the railways.

The last day of the service brought an increased demand for tickets. More than 50 people were on board the train when it left Blyth to the sound of exploding rail detonators and the blare of the train hooter.

Railway deputation waits for a call...

A SEVEN-MAN deputation is standing by to make a last-ite effort to stay the closure ...ilway passenger service ...Newcastle. Blyth ... line schedul... ...d, go a ...or

Blyth railway station, one of ten stations due for closure when the Blyth and Tyne passenger services are withdrawn.

PRESS REPORTS 1964

Fig. 8

Chapter 5

The North Tyneside Electrics

THE INTRODUCTION OF trams into Newcastle and parts of the surrounding district in 1902 took many short distance travellers away from the North Eastern Railway largely because they made frequent stops convenient for shops, homes and places of work. By the same token they were slow and cumbersome compared with trains, especially over distances of more than two or three miles.

After a careful analysis of all the facts and an appraisal of potential traffic, a decision was taken to run a frequent service of electric trains from Newcastle to the coast and back to the city. It anticipated a large volume of new passengers. Anxious not to drive more people away by modifying the existing steam timetable or by withdrawing trains altogether, the NER carried out the conversion work between trains. The system adopted was for current at 600 volts to be picked up from an outside third rail by collector shoes on the bogies. The 'live' rails were to be $3\frac{1}{4}$ inches higher than the running lines, with the centre 1 ft $7\frac{1}{4}$ ins from the inside edge of the nearer rail. They were supported on insulators. In 1936 the distance was reduced to 1 ft 4 ins and the height to 3 inches in keeping with the then standard Ministry of Transport recommendations.

The first section to be electrified for trial purposes and crew training was on the Riverside Branch between Percy Main and Carville, a distance of under three miles. This was brought into use in September 1903. Some months later on 29 March 1904, electric trains entered service between New Bridge Street (Newcastle) and Benton, four miles away. Significantly, these were the first electric trains to be operated by a British main line railway company - and it was the North Eastern Railway which took this initiative. Benton station itself, built by the Blyth & Tyne Railway Company in 1871, was just over a mile from where NER lines and the old Killingworth Waggonway crossed at right angles on the level, where George Stephenson's early railway engines trundled their loads of coal down to the Tyne long before the line to Tynemouth was built.

At the outset there were trains every fifteen minutes in each direction during the day. By the first week in June alternate trains (i.e. two an hour) were run as far as Monkseaton and by 21 June 1904 were extended to Tynemouth. Only ten days later the remainder of the route from Tynemouth to Newcastle Central via Wallsend was ready, together with the Riverside Branch, and trains were able to run right round the circuit, a distance of twenty miles. The main line section between Heaton Junction and Benton Quarry signal box, plus the two curves to Benton station and Benton East were electrified within a month, enabling trains to use them from 25 July.

The terminus at New Bridge Street was closed to passenger traffic at the end of December 1908 and the new station at Manors North was brought into use on 1 January 1909. Although a connection had been made at Manors with the lines between Newcastle and Heaton most electric trains continued to terminate at Manors North until Central to Central running for all trains was introduced on 1 March 1917. When Manors was enlarged the two parts were identified as Manors North on the left side of the Y-junction travelling from Newcastle, and Manors East on the right side. This arrangement continued until 1947 when they reverted to Manors. From the beginning the new service was a great success showing a tremendous increase in passengers carried and a considerable reduction in running costs. In 1913 over 10,000,000 passengers used the electric trains.

Current for the electrified area was supplied from the Newcastle Electric Supply Company's power station at Carville by high tension cables to railway sub-stations at Carville, Pandon Dene (near Manors), Benton, Cullercoats and, at a slightly later date, Percy Main. Another, built at Fawdon, was never equipped as the proposed electricification of the line to Ponteland did not materialise. Sufficient output was needed to run just under fifty trains at any one time. Power from the live rail passed through the motors and other apparatus to the wheels from where it was led back to the sub-stations by the track rails, all of which were suitably bonded at joints for the purpose. Where the live rails were broken - for example at level crossings, barrow crossings at stations, and at junctions, cables were passed under the ballast to join the gaps. At certain places, particularly at platform ends, the live rails had lengths of protective wooden boards fitted on either side, more perhaps as a visual reminder than a safety measure. Prominent cast iron notices warned people not to touch the elevated rails. Unfortunately dogs and cats cannot read: many an unaccompanied dog walking along the tracks met an untimely end, some by wagging their tail and touching the lethal rail!

Coaches for the 1904 service were built by the NER at York Carriage Works but the contractors, British Thomson - Houston, provided and fitted all the electrical equipment. The first order was intended to provide fifty power cars (usually referred to as *motors*) and the same number of trailers but only ninety in total were built. They were distinctive-looking vehicles, light and airy open saloons, having vertical match-boarding panels below the windows and with clerestory roofs. Each *set* consisted of three *cars* each 56½ feet over body length, with seating for 186 passengers plus a luggage or parcels area. Two motor parcels vans were also built for the conveyance of parcels and fish traffic in boxes or barrels. The luggage area, with two doors on each side, was just over forty feet in length: the compartment for fish was ten feet long and had one door on each side. These two vehicles were withdrawn from normal service in 1938 and converted to de-icing vans, used to spray a solution on to live rails to prevent ice forming.

Sheds to house the 1904 stock and to provide servicing facilities were built at Walkergate, near Heaton yard, but these were destroyed in a catastrophic fire on 11 August 1918. Thirty-four cars were totally destroyed in the blaze and many others were badly damaged. To try and maintain the service, steam sets were scrambled to supplement the electric trains that had survived, but the disaster had far-reaching consequences. It was October 1923 before new car sheds at Gosforth were ready for use. These were spacious, brick buildings covering ten through lines and two into the repair shop.

New stock supplied between 1920 and 1922 carried more modern electrical equipment and improved seating. They were given the same numbers as the coaches they replaced but did not have the clerestory roof of the earlier vehicles. After some years of good service most of these coaches were refurbished and used between Newcastle and South Shields when that route on the south side of the Tyne was electrified in 1938.

Although the fleet of electrics was supplemented as necessary and various units replaced from time to time, it was in 1937 under the LNER that the old North Eastern stock was withdrawn from North Tyneside. The new coaches were smart, modern, articulated vehicles - twin sets where two bodies were carried on three bogies, each pair being 112ft 7ins over body length. They were fitted with bucket seats and had sliding doors at the ends of each coach. 64 pairs, of four

An early style of North Eastern Railway electric train leaving Back-
worth. Notice the 'porthole' lookout in the driving compartment
and the cowhead coupling. The signal box can be seen beyond the
station on the right. (Author's collection)

The introduction of electric trains in 1904 brought an upsurge in
passengers, a fact which did not go unnoticed by the picture
postcard industry. (Author's collection)

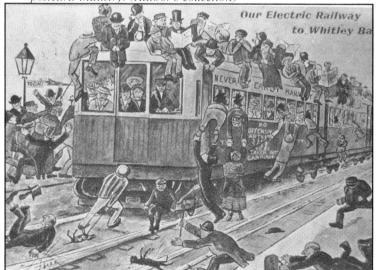

different types, were built plus four single units, two of which, as before, were for parcels traffic and fish. Whereas the 1904 stock were rated at 125 hp the new Metro Cammell motor cars were 216 hp. They were all fitted with what was called a *cowhead* coupling, as were previous types, but only the four separate units had buffers.

At this point it is appropriate to comment on what was known by local railwaymen as the *Control Set* that featured in all three eras - NER, LNER and British Railways. In the early days a rake of ten six-wheeled coaches with a motor parcel van at each end was used mainly to carry workmen to and from shipyards on the Tyne. They were fitted with jumper cables between each coach so that the motors of the rear van worked in conjunction with those at the front under the control of the driver. In 1929 the six-wheelers were replaced by six bogie coaches with separate compartments. The motor vans were superseded by those from the 1937 batch, which were attached to the train as and when necessary. The set was used on both the North Tyneside and South Tyneside electrified areas at various times until the mid 1950s after which the coaches were stored at Ponteland for some years prior to scrapping. It was referred to as the Control Set because it was put at the disposal of the Newcastle District Control for use as required apart from its scheduled runs.

During fine weekends in summer thousands of day trippers flocked to the coast and the electric trains were packed to the doors. Even with numerous extra trains, people joining at intermediate stations found great difficulty getting on even to stand and for those with prams or push chairs it was a much harder battle. To ease this problem four vans used for parcels etc were converted for use as *pram-vans* in the 1950s and were marshalled into ordinary sets to ease the congestion. Mothers, and those with them, travelled with their prams and longitudinal wooden seats were provided for them.

Coaching stock on the North Eastern Railway carried a distinctive livery and the new electric trains were no exception, even though the colours were different. From 1904 they were cream above the centre line and bright scarlet-red below. For the stock to replace those lost in the fire, however, the Company reverted to crimson lake. By contrast, the LNER repainted the vehicles in their approved teak colour which many felt did not enhance them. Consequently, before this process was completed, trains would be seen running on part of the Blyth & Tyne area in three different liveries. When the 1937 trains went into service they reverted to red and cream for the new image but only four years later this was changed to mid-blue and off-white. Two years after nationalisation the Tyneside electrics were gradually repainted in British Railways green but the single colour made them look very ordinary.

No less than 341 vehicles of various kinds, built to thirty-three styles (or *diagrams)* ran on the Tyneside electrified areas. Readers who require more information should consult "The North Eastern Electrics" by K Hoole, Oakwood Press, 1987.

To understand the sort of service provided by the electric trains north of the Tyne running between Newcastle and Tynemouth, an analysis of extracts from the 1910 NER timetable will serve as an example:-

'DOWN' LINE (weekdays)

Manors North - Benton	36 per day
Manors North - Benton, Tynemouth	
(then to Newcastle via Wallsend)	33 per day
Newcastle Central - Benton (in addition to above)	14 per day
Extra train, Newcastle - Backworth	1 per day
Expresses via south east curve from Newcastle	
to Monkseaton, Whitley Bay and Cullercoats only	5 per day
Monkseaton - Tynemouth	
(then to Newcastle via Wallsend)	71 per day (Total)
Expresses from Monkseaton, Whitley Bay, Cullercoats	
and Tynemouth to Newcastle via Wallsend	4 per day

(Note: Stopping trains called at all intermediate stations)

A comparable service was provided on the 'Up' line between Tynemouth, Benton and Manors or Newcastle. Travelling times were as follows:-

Newcastle to:

Manors	2 minutes	
Jesmond	5 minutes	
West Jesmond	8 minutes	(station opened Dec. 1990)
South Gosforth	11 minutes	
Benton	15 minutes	
Benton Square	18 minutes	
Backworth	21 minutes	
Monkseaton	28 minutes	
Whitley Bay	31 minutes	
Cullercoats	33 minutes	
Tynemouth	37 minutes	

Expresses from Newcastle to Cullercoats took 24 minutes. In NER days the round trip from Central to Central took 63 minutes but with the introduction of new stock in 1937 this was reduced by ten minutes.

Subsequently, additional stations were opened at West Monkseaton (20 March 1933) and at Longbenton (14 July 1947). The latter was built to serve the then Ministry of National Insurance offices. When the electric service was introduced in 1904 passenger trains between Monkseaton and Hartley were resumed along the Avenue Branch, as previously noted.

In general terms the frequency of trains since January 1928 has been maintained at twenty minute intervals in both directions for the full circuit, Newcastle to Newcastle. Unquestionably, the provision of regular, reliable trains to and from the city played a major part in the rapid expansion of the coastal towns for people who worked in Newcastle; in addition, the trains were a great attraction for people who wished to have a day at the seaside.

Most of the people on Tyneside were very proud of their electric trains but for some of the Cullercoats 'fisher-wives' the electrification scheme of 1904 caused great inconvenience and loss because the North Eastern Railway limited the number of trains on which they could travel. Under the old system they could carry their fish on any train but on the new trains they were limited to three for travelling to Newcastle via Wallsend from North Shields. These were the 9.25, 10.16 and 10.55 am. Those wishing to sell their fish at Jesmond were even harder hit as they could only use the 9.24 am from Tynemouth and were obliged to change at Backworth. They had to wait there "until 10.16 and frequently much later for a train to take them to their destination."

The Shields Daily News of July 20 1904 reported a public meeting where the 'fisher-wives' were told by their representative, Mr Knott, of a discussion he had had with a railway official. He was told that the Railway Company aimed to give a fast service with short stops and the trains therefore were only provided with small accommodation for luggage. They were not suitable for carrying large quantities of fish . . . and the water dripping from the fish baskets flowed into the 1st class compartments causing a smell which remained after the fish had been removed. In reply to this Mr Knott had pointed out it was one of the healthiest smells he had experienced and it was proved by the fat and healthy condition of the people at Cullercoats! The

Company, he said, was willing to give them the use of certain parcels trains of the old fashioned kind.

When the meeting was opened for discussion one fish wife, known as Long Betty, said, "We want the forst train we can catch. Some leave at five past five in the morning. The 8.30, 9.30 and 10.30 are varry good trains for us. Them that cannot get the 10.30 had better bide away." Another one, Nannie, who travelled to Jesmond, commented, "We've had the 8.20, 9.20, 10.20 and 11.20 aal wor lives . . . Dear me! Aa've a bad heed wi' fightin' wi'one of the men at Backworth this morning. It's a varry bad job for us th'electric trains ever started."

The meeting closed with the singing of the National Anthem.

Inevitably the North Tyneside electrics became time expired. They were withdrawn and replaced by slower diesel multiple units between March and June 1967. The last service on this historic route was on 17 June, leaving Newcastle Central at 6.15 pm. Many people were very sad to see them go: somehow the line to Tynemouth never seemed the same.

Fig. 9. In an attempt to boost the number of passengers, diesel trains running on the former North Tyneside electrified area carried the names of various Tyneside characters. (Early 1970s)

Chapter 6

Station to Station

THE PURPOSE OF THIS chapter is to take an imaginary trip down the line, say about the year 1950, to point out things of interest and provide additional information about places along the route not covered elsewhere in the text. We start at MANORS NORTH.

The first impression is of a rather unpretentious entrance to what appears a reasonable-sized, brick built station with covered platforms. Once past the ticket collector a passenger can go on to platform 1 for an electric train to the coast via Benton; walk alongside this Down platform past waiting rooms to reach a long footbridge spanning the station at the Newcastle end; or use the stairs and the subway to reach platform 2 (for Newcastle) and the three bay platforms. At the East side of the station main line expresses, empty stock, parcels trains, goods traffic of all kinds, light engines to and from Heaton depot, and electric trains on the Wallsend routes can be seen making frequent use of the quadruple tracks.

In former years Nestlés penny bars of chocolate machines, chewing gum dispensers and weighing machines were dotted around the station, together with a bright red, solid-looking device for printing names on thin strips of soft metal.

In the sidings alongside the bay platforms a vehicle used by the District Engineer may be seen. It was previously an 'open' saloon of the East Coast Joint Stock, with a clerestory roof.

The train we are about to board is standing at platform 3. It consists of five suburban coaches hauled by a G5 class 0-4-4 tank engine based at South Blyth. When it arrived earlier it had to push its coaches back out of the platform, move on to another track, then the coaches ran back into the station by gravity, being controlled and stopped by a brake handle in the guard's van. (It was not unknown for errors of judgement to allow the carriages to bounce off the buffer stops!)

With its water replenished from the water column at the end of the platform, a type with its own cylindrical tank, the engine is simmering quietly at the front of the train. Between platforms 2 and 3 stands the barrow hoist, very near to where an unexploded bomb damaged part of the Up platform and track during the war. Ahead, to our right, is the Guinness private siding and loading bay.

The bay platform at which our train is standing has been used in the past for exhibitions of rolling stock. The one held there in 1939 featured Patrick Stirling's Great Northern Railway locomotive No. 1 - an elegant greyhound with single driving wheels eight feet in diameter. There were also some six-wheeled coaches as used on 'The Flying Scotsman' express at one time.

The train moves out. Once under the bridge it crosses over to the Down line and starts the laborious climb up gradients of 1:87, 1:72, 1:81 and 1:72, as indicated on gradient posts at the side of the track. There are high retaining walls on either side, with Manors North signal box protruding from the one on the left. Reception 'roads' for goods traffic run alongside the electrified lines, to our right.

On the right also is New Bridge Street Goods Station, the building still largely a shell after bomb damage. In 1923 the goods yard handled all machinery and vehicles for the Royal Agricultural Show held on the Town Moor. Almost opposite is the former terminus of the Blyth & Tyne Railway which had four platforms and five sidings. The platforms were taken out and the area is now a coal depot with seven mineral sidings plus two coal-drops. The former Station Master's house there became offices of the District Engineer.

There is a brief easing of the gradient as the train struggles through JESMOND station, built of stone by the Blyth & Tyne Railway. The solid, stone bridges over the line at either end of the station are also typical of their original owner and one still retains its "B & T 1864" plate.

By the time WEST JESMOND is reached the sturdy engine is no longer having to work so hard: again it does not stop and proceeds towards SOUTH GOSFORTH under more B & T bridges. Well ahead of the station (the name of which was changed from 'Gosforth' in March 1905) is a post bearing a white, metal diamond with a broad red border. This is one of many such signs on the electrified area which tell drivers of electric trains to shut off power and coast. Before we enter the station we may see a loop running alongside the Up line. This was where the autocar for the Ponteland Branch stood between turns, up to June 1929. The metal base of the water column is there as a reminder. In one of the allotments nearby is the light green body from an old four-wheeled coach, well bedded into the grass, ending its days as a garden shed - or, perhaps, as a haven of peace for the gardener.

The station gardens here were well cared for at one time. At the far end of the station is a typical NER footbridge connecting the platforms. Once under the road bridge the lines divide, those on the left lead to the Ponteland Branch (opened for passengers in June 1905) and to Gosforth Car Sheds, the west end. Our train, having slowed for the tight-curve, takes the right hand side of the Y-junction. On our left can be seen several electric trains standing outside the sheds. From time to time one of the two electric locomotives for use between Manors and the Newcastle Quayside may also be noticed. These have a central cab, from which the body slopes towards the buffer beams, and are carried on two 4-wheeled bogies. Built in 1904, they were originally numbered 1 and 2 but eventually became 26500 and 26501 under British Railways. The signal box controlling the traffic into and out of the car sheds at the Longbenton end is South Gosforth East, a very high cabin with a commanding view. The junction there also joins up with the Ponteland Branch to make a triangle. Once off the curve our train crosses over a road. It was here that two railwaymen were killed when their engine plunged from the bridge in December 1923 (see page 128). The cast iron bridge side opposite the site of the mishap remains as another reminder of the Blyth & Tyne Railway.

On our right is the Lucozade factory with half a dozen covered vans in the siding alongside and almost immediately we go through LONGBENTON station, the last to be built on this branch. "The Ministry" sprawls fingers of buildings across its own site on one side while on the other is a large housing estate.

The train has picked up speed now and weaves its way under more bridges on the approach to BENTON. The lower quadrant outer home signal, protecting a crossover, is very high so that it can be seen by drivers, well clear of obstructing bridges. Because this signal is so tall there is a repeater arm at a much lower level, useful if a train has been stopped as the driver can draw up almost level with the signal and still see it. At the east end of the Down platform, ahead of our train, is one of the more significant features of Benton - the triple junction. On the right the south west curve leads to the main line south at Benton Quarry; the tracks in the centre are to Backworth and beyond; those to the left form the north west curve which joins the main line north at Benton North box. These junctions are controlled by a gantry of three home and three distant signals, one for each

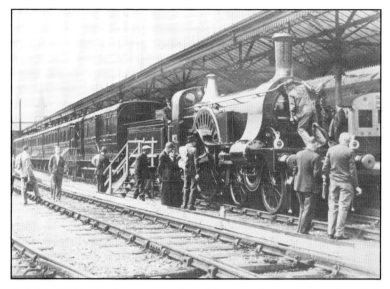

Patrick Stirling's elegant number 1 locomotive with a train of 6-wheeled coaches, brought out of retirement, are shown on display at Manors. The single driving wheel is 8 feet in diameter. The loco is still in the national collection. (Author's collection)

route, with the pair for the north being NER lower quadrant types. By contrast, the rest are modern upper quadrant signals. On the south west curve, in spite of a steep, curved gradient, any runaway vehicles would be diverted into long sand drags before they reached the main line. The Benton signal box, too, is elevated - 38 stairs from ground to entrance.

After passing the sub-station on our right the train quickly crosses above the main line at right angles on an overbridge, alongside which is a pedestrian bridge, old but still in use. Half a mile further on the south east curve trails in from our right. A J27 with empty coal hoppers is standing at the signal, which is at danger, waiting for a 'path' to follow us along the line, probably to Ashington. Just beside the junction at Benton East signal box can be seen a short section of wall which formed part of a platform on the former Blyth & Tyne station called Forest Hall. It is now only a matter of seconds before the unmistakable rattle of wheels tells us we have crossed the old Killingworth Waggonway, now an NCB route to the Tyne. An electric train passes on the Up line. Some of its passengers will be waiting for

us at the next station. Two bomb craters near the line here remained
for several years.

BACKWORTH is the first scheduled stop since the train left Manors
North. It is approached downhill, with patches of heather growing on
the embankments. Another National Coal Board line crosses above
the station platforms which are on a slight curve. A small cast sign

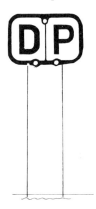

showing the letters "DP" (found on many
former NER stations) stands for *distance point,*
from which distances are measured. There is
no truth in the old railwaymen's tale that it
stands for 'Dead Porter buried here'! The
replacement booking office was built on an
overbridge bordering the road. On the opposite side of the road was the signal box but it
was demolished when a new one was built at
ground level. It is here that the tracks divide:
the electrified lines to Tynemouth curve off
and dip to the right but our train will face the
rising gradient and an S-curve to the left. The
coaches give a definite lurch as we leave the reverse curve, then we
clatter over the crossings of the double track NCB line to Percy Main,
join the junction at Earsdon and immediately jig across another
colliery line at right angles. It is now a falling gradient and the train
quickly gathers speed.

At the next signal box, HOLYWELL, is the first set of level crossing
gates. There will be several others before Newbiggin is reached, but
significantly there are none between Newcastle and Tynemouth via
Benton. The old goods station, an office and a small warehouse on
a very short platform built from railway sleepers, is hardly noticed and
once over the crossing a facing junction swings left from the BR lines,
across those of the NCB, to collieries at Burradon. It was along there
that a broken rail caused fifteen or so empty coal wagons to shudder
off the track in the early 1940s. The difference between *railway*
maintained and *colliery* track between Holywell and SEGHILL is
obvious, even from the train. This section, though, has historical
significance because it was here the two Timothy Hackworth
engines, No. 1 *Samson* and No. 2 *John* worked on the Seghill Railway
from 1840. The train has to slow down as it approaches Seghill South
signal box in order to pass safely through the crossover on to the Up
line, though on Sundays the trains run past the station and shunt back

into the platform. Because of the four tracks there was not room to put a platform on the 'Down' side. The dilapidated hut serving as a signal box for the colliery traffic stands on a base of old sleepers. The station at Seghill is a very modest affair but the signal box is a replacement for one hit by a land-mine early in the war. Once back on the Down line the train goes over the level crossing before the track curves gently right. On the left are the sidings serving Seghill Colliery and the brickyard. We no longer have NCB tracks alongside us. This area of the Northumberland coal field has huge heaps of colliery waste and from the train can be seen large 'buckets' moving at intervals on the aerial ropeway, the empty ones hanging upside down as they return to be re-loaded.

Shortly afterwards we arrive at SEATON DELAVAL where a new station was approved in 1884. The NER milepost tells us we are 10 miles from Manors. Between mileposts are others showing $^1/_4$, $^1/_2$ and $^3/_4$ in figures and with one, two or three triangles as a further visual guide.

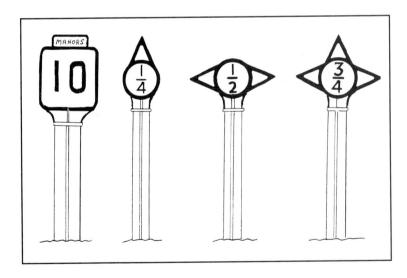

The booking office and a waiting room are on the overbridge as at Backworth but here the Station Master's house is on the Down platform, with the porters' room and a small warehouse underneath two of the bedrooms. There are also a small waiting room and toilets on the Down platform. Just before they are reached, as the train enters the station, there is a low, grassy slope where a wild rabbit once made its nesting burrow only a yard away from the platform surface. Unfortunately, her young ones were dug out by a marauding dog. Nearby, in one of the station lamps, a pair of blue tits nested for several years. The line into the colliery is on the left, just under the bridge.

When a horse box was brought to this station by passenger train it was placed next to the engine. The coaches were left in the Down platform while the engine drew forward with the horse box. It then had to reverse through the crossover on to the Up line, pull forward into the siding, shunt back again into the short cattle dock and detach the truck. The engine then had four moves to rejoin its train. Horse boxes could carry up to three horses in removable padded stalls; there was a grooms' compartment with lifting hatches so the animals could be checked and fed on the journey. Horses on this line were not usually accompanied but arrangements could be made for railway staff to feed them en route if necessary. At the other end of these vehicles was a compartment for hay, bedding or tackle.

On one occasion, about 1942, the Gateshead breakdown train was returning to depot through Seaton Delaval when the train had to be stopped on account of a damaged axle on the crane. It was shunted off at the end of the siding and left for a week before another crane was brought in from York to lift out the damaged bogie, leaving the Gateshead crane propped up on sleepers. When the bogie was brought back some days later and re-fitted, both cranes left together.

A railwayman was injured here whilst working on a ballast train. It is said he was on one of the wagons which was being tipped when he lost his grip and fell through the bottom doors with the ballast.

The weight of a wartime barricade which was built on the bridge itself caused problems of subsidence and the whole structure had to be supported from below by hefty girders and packing, thus closing the Up line. Single line working, with all trains using the Down line, remained in operation between Hartley and Seaton Delaval for a considerable time before points were installed just ahead of the obstruction, and all Up trains were brought through the Down platform, rejoining the Up line through a crossover put in at the south end of the station.

The next station we stop at is HARTLEY, on a tight curve. Check rails help the wheels of vehicles to negotiate the bend and prevent them leaving the track. The first station here, on a different site, was called

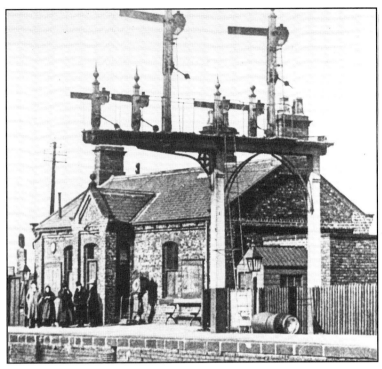

Seghill station circa 1900 (T Allan collection)

HARTLEY PIT. It served the ill-fated Hester Colliery where a calamity in 1862 caused the deaths of more than 200 men and boys. Both stations, however, were built by the Blyth & Tyne Railway Company. As the train pulls away we can see the single track Avenue Branch to Monkseaton. There is now a straight run along to NEWSHAM.

After Newsham South level crossing the double track becomes four as there is an *independent* (or long loop) on either side to Newsham North. We pass two small reservoirs, one each side, which attract migrating swans from time to time. Beside the one on the Down line are two water tanks resting on stone towers from where water is pumped to water columns. By now the sidings and lines that handle most of the interchange traffic for Blyth and the staiths are on our right. Quite a number of 21-ton coal hoppers can be seen. Some of the buffer stops at the end of sidings are built from sections of rail. Just as we are about to enter the station there are two ex North Eastern Railway six-wheeled snowploughs standing in the short spur near the signal box, still carrying a faded, blue livery. They are coupled with their blades outwards but when in use there are usually two strong engines coupled tender to tender in between them. When going to clear the line of deep snow they are signalled as express passenger trains and take priority over other traffic. Workmen who may be needed to dig out trains travel in the van part of these vehicles. It is quite a spectacular sight to see a snowplough train tackle drifts at speed though it is not unknown for a derailment to occur when hard-packed, frozen snow under the blade has lifted the wheels.

Passengers for Blyth change at Newsham and use the tiled subway to reach the other two platforms. A three coach push-and-pull train with a G5 loco at the rear has been waiting in the branch platform for our train to arrive. It is a good opportunity to have a look at Blyth then catch a later train to complete our journey to Newbiggin. The subway at Newsham was totally filled with water when severe flooding caused havoc at Blyth and surrounding areas in October 1900.

The train which brought us from Manors leaves the Down platform just as another coal train rumbles through on the opposite line, the buffers of the wagons crushing together as the engine slows them down before entering the sidings. This coal is for export at New Blyth. With a pert toot on the whistle the train we are now in sets off pushed from behind, passing the tracks which run alongside the golf course on their way to the staiths. We pass through more gates at Isabella where a single track leads to another colliery. Here, in 1868, a passenger train collided with a stationary coal train. In a few minutes, as the track curves to the right over Blyth Crossing, we can see the engine sheds on our left and we slowly enter BLYTH terminus.

Blyth has several reminders of its early association with railways. About three miles from the town centre a small section of embankment from the original Plessey Waggonway (OS reference NZ 276791) can still be seen from the road and only a short distance from it is what remains of the double line of hawthorn bushes that often edged a waggonway. Plessey Road covers part of that ancient route, and the name of Ballast Hill (where ballast for ships was kept) survives on a building near the Quayside. Almost opposite the station entrance is a public house appropriately called *The Blyth & Tyne*. On the Cambois side of the river, Worsdell Terrace reminds us of two brothers of that name who were, in succession, Locomotive Superintendents of the North Eastern Railway.

Gresley V3 2-6-2T number 67646 on a stopping passenger train at Seaton Delaval in the early 1960s. Work on the overbridge requires the use of a look-out, seen standing on the platform holding a warning horn. (J M Fleming)

Ashington station circa 1920 with a passenger train from Newbiggin entering the station on the 'Up' line. (Taken from a postcard: L G Charlton collection)

In May 1933, five years after a similar event, a Charity Exhibition was held by the LNER at Blyth in aid of the Thomas Knight Memorial Hospital, Cancer Research, and the NER Cottage Homes. The Exhibition consisted of many of the latest types of engines and carriages plus interesting signalling devices and assorted wagons. The rolling stock included an A3 'Pacific' type express locomotive, number 2579 *Dick Turpin* in lined, apple-green livery, a Hunt class engine called *The Meynell;* a diesel electric coach named *Lady Hamilton;* a West Riding Pullman coach; an East Coast third class saloon; together with a snowplough, platelayers' petrol trolley, a refrigerated van and a 'Protrol' trolley wagon. The Exhibition was supervised by Mr R C Douglas, the Station Master, capably assisted by his staff. At intervals The Blyth LNER Prize Band rendered selections. (This band was successful in several competitions. In April 1932, for example, it gained 3rd place out of 19 competing bands at Chester-le-Street when the test piece was 'Beautiful Britain'.)

Before joining the train back to Newsham we have time to walk along the platform to see some of the wagons standing in the goods yard. On this occasion there are some of the new 16-ton steel mineral wagons, a few wooden open wagons, two double bolsters, a long tube wagon loaded with pipes, and several vans. There are also four bogie parcel vans. In the past the odd 'Pooley Van' may have been seen - a mobile workshop for testing and correcting large weighing machines which could weigh full wagons.

Every so often a Painters' van is in a siding nearest the station. These vans, converted coaches really, visit every station on a rota basis to enable a team of railway painters carry out redecoration. At one time redundant four or six-wheeled coaches or luggage vans were used for this purpose around the District.

One of the old stable blocks in the goods yard area was converted into a garage for motor vehicles at some time in the past.

On the opposite side we can look across at the six-road engine shed. The coaling stage stands aloft and wagons of coal have to be pushed up the steep ramp. From them the coal is shovelled into what can best be described as large scuttles on wheels and tipped into the tenders or bunkers of engines below. It is a hard, dirty job at any time.

Returning to Newsham, our train from Blyth has to run past the Branch platform, stop, and shunt back as there has never been a facing crossover at the Blyth end of that platform. This has always brought consternation to some passengers not familiar with the working, particularly during the war-time blackout. In the early 1900s there were no less than 39 trains a day in each direction between Blyth and Newsham, 43 on Saturdays.

Looking along the track northwards it can be seen there is a single siding on the Down side with a small warehouse. On the Up side there used to be a siding with coal cells between the station and Plessey Road signal box but this was all removed some years ago. One other thing which may be of interest at Newsham is what the local railwaymen call *the cage*, situated a few yards from Newsham North cabin. It is a number of steel 'rods' in a frame just above ground level, worked by various wires from levers in the signal box as a miniature interlocking device to prevent conflicting signals being pulled off at the same time. Normally all points and signals are interlocked under the cabin floor. This means it is not possible for a signal to show clear if the points are wrongly set: similarly if a signal is *off* points cannot be changed until it is put back to danger. According to the Station Master there is only one other 'cage' of this type in the country.

Our train is now approaching. This time it is hauled by one of the smart, Gresley V3 2-6-2- tank locomotives which are only used on two return trips each weekday.

Just before we reach BEBSIDE there is a splodge of buildings and sidings used for coal from an open-cast site not far away, which provides quite a lot of traffic for rail. This station was originally called Cowpen Lane.

One would not expect to find information relating to railways in a School Log Book but these entries appeared in one from Bebside Colliery Boys' School:-

11th Feb. 1874	Left School at 2 pm to attend the funeral of the late Mr Telford, Station Master.
21st June 1875	Alexander Cheyne, having been one afternoon at school last week, has gone to assist the Station Master.
15th Dec. 1876	2 boys absent, one has had one of his legs cut off by an engine, the other had his left arm broken. A number of boys are absent carrying coals. (The boy who lost a leg at Sleekburn returned to school on 19.3.1877.)
25th Jan. 1878	A thin school today. Children carrying coals.
2nd June 1880	Mr Bainbridge was at school today to announce

that Messrs Rutherford (Station Master) and Foster (Store Keeper) were to pay fees for their children.

Shortly after leaving this station there is a slight deviation of the track as it approaches the viaduct high over the River Blyth. This indicates a new one was built alongside the original wooden one. A picture in a local newspaper of 1929 showed work in progress, with four huge, steel sections, nearly 80 ft long and 6 ft high already in position. Across this bridge and on our left are the Furnace Way sidings controlled by Bedlington South 'box, as is the entrance to the 'A' Pit and the Doctor Pit. Just over the level crossing is a footbridge climbing over the two tracks and tucked in beside it are the remains of an old, colliery signal box. BEDLINGTON has only one through platform hence Down passenger trains have to pass on to the Up line before they reach the crossing. They draw up well forward so that the engine can take water. The water column there is the type that has a bulbous end about the size of a football opposite the flexible hose, an LNER design. For years starlings have nested in it. When an engine pulls up for water and the column is turned, the bird flies off and returns when the train has gone. It never bothers when the engines are just passing in spite of all the chuffs and hisses.

The bay platform was for connecting trains to Newbiggin when Morpeth was the terminus. Extra trains between Bedlington and Newbiggin (jocularly called by staff *The Newbiggin Pullman*) were run on fine weekends in the summer and for this purpose half a dozen old coaches were stabled in the bay. After their last trip the doors on the platform side were locked with a carriage key otherwise they became a favourite venue for courting couples. If, however, the porter was late locking up it was not unknown for a couple to be inadvertently(?) locked in a compartment and have to clamber out through the window or face a long drop on to the ballast on the other side!

Bedlington, of course, is famous for its Iron Works but it is not generally known that Sir Daniel Gooch, Locomotive Superintendent of the Great Western Railway, was born there: another contributor from the North East to Britain's early railways.

From Bedlington the tracks dip to West Sleekburn cabin where there are more collieries and on our right is the junction to North Blyth for the coal staiths and the engine sheds. Half a mile or so ahead is the junction for North Blyth from the Ashington side. We cross another viaduct, this time over the River Wansbeck, and make a short stop at NORTH SEATON.

At ASHINGTON the platforms are on a slight curve below road level. Former North Eastern Railway and LNER barrows can be seen. A 1917 plan of proposed alterations to the station shows platforms 572 ft long extended by 112 ft which meant some track and points had to be moved slightly. The intended site for the Station Master's house was indicated, adjoining the station buildings on the Up platform. There was to be a stable and a stableman's house though in order to keep the footpath to the latter within the NER boundary a siding would have to be eased across a little. The booking office also dealt with parcels forwarded and left luggage but a new parcels office for received traffic was included in the plan. The general waiting room on the Up platform was shown as 40 ft x 20 ft. There were separate ladies' rooms for first class and third class passengers but only a first class one for gentlemen. The goods warehouse had a through track and had bays for two rullies. Nearby in the goods yard was a small Police cabin. Horses and prize cattle were unloaded at the end of the Down platform. Fish traffic was stored under the stairs of a footbridge.

Once passed Woodhorn signal box it is single line to NEWBIGGIN where the main platform has a crossover to release engines. This platform when built was approximately 600 ft long and the bay (shown on plans as the Excursion Platform) some 360 ft in length. Alterations proposed in 1902 extended both platforms by 130 ft. Track had to be altered slightly to achieve this. In the goods yard was a small warehouse with loading dock and a 1-ton crane, also a small turntable. Extra sidings were provided in February 1913 which meant further changes in the track layout.

The V3 has already run round its train and now awaits its scheduled departure back to Manors.

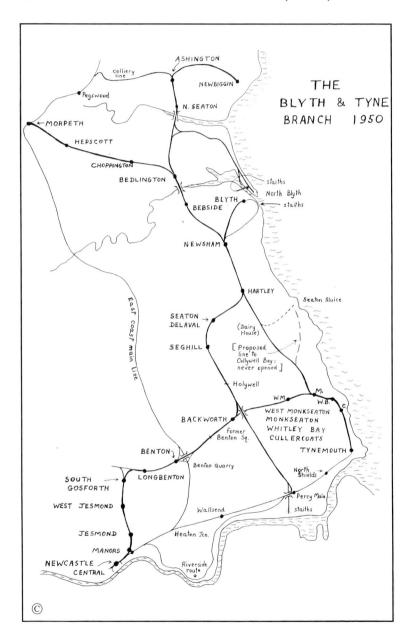

Fig. 10

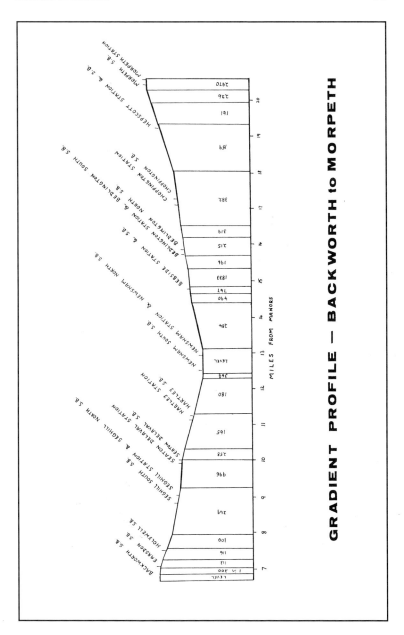

Fig 11

Chapter 7

Newcastle Central Station

IT IS BEYOND THE scope of this book to consider the development of Newcastle as a major railway centre, nevertheless it is appropriate to look in some detail at its role and organisation at a specific time in its history. The information given below is taken from notes prepared for a Short Works Course for Public & Grammar School Boys in 1960 and is produced in its entirety by courtesy of British Rail.

VISIT TO NEWCASTLE CENTRAL STATION:
STATION MASTER Mr W H CAMPBELL

Newcastle is fortunate in that it is one of the few large cities in the country with only one main railway station and Newcastle Central Station is also scheduled as a building of special architectural merit. It is one of the largest and most important stations in the country and in 1958 it handled 14,665,968 passengers, more than any other station in the country outside London.

The station buildings were designed by the Newcastle architect, John Dobson, and were opened by Queen Victoria and Prince Albert in August 1850. In 1871 the station was enlarged by the construction of an island platform on the south side, bringing the total number of platforms to nine. In 1877 a further development increased the number of platforms to twelve and the final enlargement was made in 1894 when the East End Concourse and the Royal Station Hotel were opened. There are now fifteen platforms, of which only three are through platforms and the remainder are terminal bays. The longest platform is No. 8 which is 445 yards long and the shortest is No. 12, which is only 145 yards long.

The High Level Bridge, carrying both rail and road traffic on a double-deck structure over the River Tyne at the east end of Newcastle Central, was opened in 1849 and the King Edward Bridge, which carries rail traffic only, at the west end of Newcastle Central, was opened in 1906. Until 1906 all through East Coast trains had to reverse at Newcastle.

The North Tyneside Area was electrified in 1904 and the South Tyneside line in 1938. Nos. 1 to 6 platforms at the east end are equipped with the electrified third rail but in practice the North Tyneside electric trains mainly use Nos. 1 to 3 platforms and the South Tyneside trains use No. 6 platform. No. 4 platform is mainly used by trains to and from Alnwick, Berwick and the north. No. 5 platform is used by the diesel services to and from Sunderland and Middlesbrough. No. 7 platform is used for parcels traffic and also for local boat trains to and from Tyne Commission Quay in connection with the Norwegian services, which sail almost daily during the summer. At the West end Nos. 11 to 13 platforms are used mainly for parcels traffic and nos. 14 and 15 platforms for the diesel services to Hexham and Carlisle. The introduction of diesel services has considerably reduced the amount of shunting and the number of light engine movements at both ends of the station, with beneficial results on the working.

The three main line platforms, Nos. 8, 9 and 10, can be worked in either direction, but the existence of only three through platforms (and no terminal platforms of any length except No. 4) is a considerable disadvantage at exceptionally busy periods, when delays waiting for platforms at Newcastle become almost inevitable if mainline trains are running out of course. In addition to three through platform lines, there are four through goods lines on the south side of the station.

Completely new electric lighting of the latest type, was installed on all the platforms and concourses in 1958.

Colour light signalling was introduced throughout the station in 1956-57. On 12 April 1959 a new Signal Box, situated on Nos. 9 and 10 platforms, was opened, replacing four existing signal boxes at Newcastle, Nos. 1, 2 and 3 and Manors. The new signal box is so designed that it can be extended at a later date to include the area at present worked by eight other signal boxes. The new installation is a Route Relay Interlocking Colour-light System, similar to that which has been operating successfully at York for about eight years. The points and signals are power operated and controlled through route switches by the signalmen. The routes set up by the signalmen are indicated by lighted strips on a panel in the signal box and the train automatically indicates its progress by further lights on the panel.

The new signal box controls 10 miles of track by 94 colour light signals and 87 ground subsidiary signals, through 641 route switches and 132 point switches. By comparison, the three displaced electro-pneumatic signal boxes at Newcastle and the one control-panel signal box at Manors had 538 miniature levers and 34 switches respectively, with 330 semaphore signals (before the recent installation of colour light signals).

The working of trains in and out of Newcastle Central is outlined in a printed Station Working Booklet which is published with each issue of the timetable and is amended from day to day as necessary for temporary and special working arrangements. The Assistant Station Master on duty, who is normally located in the signal box, is responsible for the platforming of trains and, in the event of out of course running or an emergency, he makes arrangements for altered platform working by giving instructions to the Traffic Regulator. He also keeps in close touch with the District Control Office, the Platform Inspectors and the Ticket Collectors by telephone and, of course, advises the Station Announcer of any altered platform arrangements. This function has been considerably simplified by the introduction of one new signal box in place of the three previous boxes.

The majority of main line trains starting or terminating at Newcastle are stabled at Heaton Carriage Sidings but a number of additional trains, particularly in the Summer, are stabled at Scotswood Bridge Sidings. All the electric trains and most of the diesel trains are stabled at Gosforth Car Sheds, but the West Line diesel trains are also stabled at Scotswood Bridge Sidings. Locomotives are changed at Newcastle on almost all the through East Coast expresses and the engines are provided from either Heaton or Gateshead Motive Power Depots.

A very large quantity of parcels traffic is handled at Newcastle Central and it is most important that parcels trains arriving at the main platforms should be dealt with expeditiously in order to clear the platforms as quickly as possible for the arrival of more important passenger trains. Out of the 11,000 parcels which are handled at Newcastle Central on an average day, only about 40% are to or from Newcastle proper and the remaining 60% are for transfer from one train to another at Newcastle. All town traffic has to be hauled to or from the Parcels Office at the East End of the station by barrow tractors and, except for urgent and perishable traffic, all transfer traffic also has to be hauled to and from the Top Deck at the East End for sorting, as there is no room for this work in the centre of the station. There is an electrified dock at the East End, adjoining the Parcels Office, for the electric parcels vans on the North Tyneside Electrified Area and also for fish traffic. At the West end there are three docks, which are mainly used for fruit and flower traffic and also for the car sleeper services to Dover, Exeter and Inverness during the Summer.

In addition to the railway parcels traffic, there is a heavy town and transfer traffic in parcels post, which is handled by railway staff on behalf of the Post Office and there is an underground subway connected by hoists to the main platforms, direct from the station to the GPO Sorting Office. Post Office staff take letter mails direct to and from the trains.

The comparative numbers of passenger trains dealt with at Newcastle Central per day are as follows:-

	WINTER WEEKDAY	SUMMER WEEKDAY	FIRST SATURDAY IN AUGUST
Starting	237	259	253
Terminating	247	267	284
Through	37	44	67
	521	570	604

Straddling tracks at the east end of Newcastle Central, No. 1 signal box gave signalmen a commanding view of the station and its approaches. (Author's collection)

The number of staff under the supervision of the Station Master, Newcastle, at present totals 569 who are employed in the following grades:-

Assistant Station Masters	3
Traffic Regulators	3
Clerks	22
Station Inspectors	26
Foremen	8
Porters (all grades)	218
Ticket Collectors (including "Travelling T Cs")	47
Passenger Guards	116
Goods Guards	1
Train Attendants	6
Carriage Servicemen and women	22
Shunters	23
Lavatory & Waiting Room Attendants	9
Office Cleaners	6
Signalmen & Relief Signalmen	57
Signal Lampmen	2
TOTAL	569

At large stations such as Newcastle it is the practice to have separate Passenger and Parcels Agents in charge of the purely commercial functions which are performed in the Booking Office, Enquiry Office, Parcels Office, Left Luggage Office etc, and the staff in these offices do not come under the supervision of the Station Master.

Booking and Enquiry Offices - Passenger Agent, Mr A E Evans.

The Passenger Agent, who is in charge of the Main Booking and Enquiry Office, the Seat Reservation Office and the East-end Booking Office, has a staff of 43 clerks in winter, but 74 in summer.

The Main Booking Office, which is open continuously, deals with all bookings except those for the North Tyneside Electrified Area. There are seven booking windows, allocated as follows:-

(1) and (2) Excursions, Season Tickets, Dogs, Bicycles, Horses and other livestock.

(3) North Main - Stations to Berwick and Scotland.

West Line - Stations to Carlisle and beyond (including Ireland via Stranraer - Larne).

(4) Spare (for busy periods).

(5) South Local - Branches and Main-line stations to York.

(6) and (7) South Main - Stations beyond York, The Midlands, South of England, Wales and Ireland (other than via Stranraer - Larne).

The Enquiry Office, which is in the Main Booking Office, deals with train and general enquiries, postal telegrams (despatched to GPO by pneumatic tube), Continental enquiries, reservations and ticket issues, CTAC inclusive tours, Car Sleeper Services, excess fares, etc. The Telephone Desk, which has four GPO telephone lines, deals with telephone enquiries as well as personal applications for sleeping berth reservations throughout the country. Newcastle is the controlling station for sleeping berth reservations on all up East Coast sleeping car expresses south of Edinburgh, and the sleeping car lists are prepared nightly.

The Seat Reservation Office, which is separate from the Main Booking Office, deals with Ordinary and Pullman Seat Reservations on all reserved-seat trains starting from Newcastle, as well as accepting applications for seat reservations on any other reserved-seat train throughout the country. At the peak holiday weekends in July and August, individual seat reservations are suspended on most of the trains starting from Tyneside and Wearside and replaced by a special system of Block Seat Regulation, by which the number of passengers admitted to a regulated train is limited to the number of seats on that train (second class seats, four-a-side).

During the summer months, British Railways have a female clerk on board each of the Bergen Line vessels which run between the Tyne Commission Quay and Norway. She gives train and general information, issues British and Irish rail tickets and also makes seat reservations on the boat trains for passengers during the voyage from Norway.

There is an Information Inspector, who moves about Newcastle Station concourse to give train service information and assist the travelling public generally. He also attends at Tyne Commission Quay when the vessels of the Bergen and Fred Olsen Lines arrive, to assist disembarking passengers. The Information Inspector wears a distinctive maroon-coloured uniform. During the summer months there are two Information Inspectors, who cover early and late turns of duty.

The East-end Booking Office, which is open from 6.00 am to 12.00 midnight deals with local bookings to stations on the North and South Tyneside electrified areas, the Blyth and Tyne area and the Sunderland line. There are four booking windows, but only two are in use normally, the other two being used on busy summer days. This office is equipped with four electrically-operated Westinghouse-Garrard Rapid-printing and Ticket-issuing machines, one for each window. There are 25 series of tickets on each of the two main machines and 10 series on each of the spares. Tickets are printed, dated and delivered by pressing the appropriate button.

The following figures indicate the amount of business done in 1959:-

No. of Ordinary Tickets issued (Main Booking Office)   1,442,705
No. of Ordinary Tickets issued (East-end Office)   1,973,355
No. of Season Tickets issued (Both Offices)   3,783
No. of Platform Tickets issued   334,560
No. of Continental Tickets issued   2,001
No. of Ordinary Seats reserved   187,084
No. of Pullman Seats reserved   27,568
No. of Sleeping Berths reserved   38,751

The Parcels Office - Parcels Agent, Mr A R Middleton

The Parcels Office is situated mainly in the arches underneath the East-end of Newcastle Central Station. Access to the station is provided by two electric hoists, each of 2 tons capacity and also by a staircase at the far end of the East-end dock next to No. 1 Platform.

Received traffic is brought on barrows from the platforms to a sorting enclosure, known as the Top Deck, at the end of the East-end Dock. Here the traffic is sorted by Parcels Office staff into the various delivery rounds before it is taken down No. 1 hoist on barrows to the Parcels Office, where the traffic is taken to the various recesses allocated to specific delivery rounds. The parcels are then entered on delivery sheets before being taken to the cartage area for loading on to road vehicles for delivery.

Forwarded traffic is brought into the Parcels Office both by British Railways road vehicles and also by the traders concerned. After the parcels have been weighed and charged, they are taken on barrows up No. 2 hoist to the Top Deck, where the traffic is then sorted by the Station Master's staff before despatch to the various platforms, together with the transfer traffic from one platform to another which is also sorted at the same place.

The cartage area at the front of the Parcels Office is 65 feet across at the widest point, tapering to about 20 feet at the other end. The area is severely restricted for the amount of parcels traffic carted at Newcastle and also leads into a rather congested street, so that the movement of road vehicles is particularly difficult at busy times. The cartage area is equipped with two lifting blocks, one of 20 cwts and the other of 10 cwts capacity, as well as a platform weighing machine of 30 cwts capacity.

There are 24 road vehicles attached to Newcastle Parcels Office, of which 8 are battery electric vans and the remainder are petrol-driven. They cover a daily collection and delivery area of about 90 square miles with a population of about 500,000. About 90% of the parcels traffic is carted by British Railways road vehicles and the remainder by traders' own vehicles. Most of the fruit and flower traffic, however, is collected by the merchants' vehicles.

The following figures give some indication of the parcels traffic handled on an average day:-

No. of parcels forwarded	2,000
No. of parcels received	3,000
No. of fruit and flower packages received: Winter	2,000
Summer	9,000

(The number of parcels forwarded and received on peak days is about 50% more than the average.)

The Parcels Agent is also in charge of the Left Luggage Office in the Main Concourse, as well as the two banks of Automatic Luggage Lockers, of which there are 24 in the Main Concourse and 16 at the East-end. The Parcels Agent's staff at present totals 120, as follows:-

Clerks	37	Vanlads	20
Townsman	1	Porters	33
Cartage Foreman	1		———
Office Cleaner	1		120
Motor Drivers	27		———

The total amount of parcels traffic handled at Newcastle in 1959 was as follows:-

No. of parcels and PLA* forwarded	612,694	
No. of parcels and PLA* received	918,034	
Tonnage of fish forwarded	107	tons
No. of packages of fish, fruit, flowers, etc. received	1,180,391	
No. of Cloakroom deposits	208,445	
No. of Automatic Locker deposits	30,859	

* Paid Luggage in Advance

Chapter 8

Goods Traffic

IN 1881 APPROXIMATELY 70,000,000 tons of goods were conveyed on the railways of Great Britain and this figure grew rapidly until road transport was well established. As common carriers the railways could cope with anything -

from barley to bicycles and boats,
from fish to furniture and fruit,
from tar to telegraph poles and traction engines,
from milk to machinery and mohair.

Even complete circus trains and travelling theatres posed no real problems, the railways would do it.

They did so by building huge goods stations and sidings at main centres all of which handled loads to and from smaller places. These, in turn, acted as receiving and distribution centres for the areas they served. Most stations, even small ones, had a goods yard and warehouse, the design and accommodation of which were determined by the amount of traffic they were expected to handle. By the early 1920s well over a hundred railway companies shared the task of transporting loads all over the country in a highly complex system which took thousands of staff to administer, locally and at the Railway Clearing House, to ensure each company was properly paid for carrying another's goods or for wagons detained in their territory.

Fully loaded wagons travelling from one centre to another had a big advantage over mixed loads for several destinations, but in fact a large proportion of traffic handled was in small consignments. The North Eastern Railway operated a system of *through* wagons or vans from one point to another where the loads justified this but used what they called *road vans* for conveying goods for several stations on the same section of line. When the train stopped at each station served by a particular van or vans, staff took out what was intended for it and put in anything that the instructions permitted. The Company issued lists of road vans and the stations they served. *Smalls* traffic - individual pieces or a small number of boxes, crates, barrels, etc. - were sent from stations and depots in *tranship vans* to a tranship centre such as Gateshead. By their nature these items would have to be handled several times during their journey as they were transferred from one truck to another. The North Eastern built special vans for these purposes capable of carrying 15 tons each. Similar in design, road vans and tranship vans were 27 ft long over body but the former had two doors on each side for rapid loading and unloading whereas the tranship vans had only one. There was also a fleet of 25-ton capacity bogie vans though much of the merchandise was carried in ordinary open wagons and covered vans of various kinds. Special vehicles were available for particular loads such as cattle, meat, plate glass, large pulley wheels, sheets of steel and agricultural implements. Before goods trains were fitted with brakes operated from the engine their average speed would be only 25 mph.

Morpeth will serve as a useful example of the organisation of a typical goods station. It had facilities for handling livestock, furniture vans, carriages, portable engines and machines on wheels, horse boxes and prize cattle vans, in addition to general commodities. It also had a ten-ton capacity crane for assisting with larger loads in the goods yard. Horses were used to help with shunting but two other methods used with locomotives are often confused. In *loose shunting* a small number of wagons, usually not more than five at a time, were given a push by the locomotive then allowed to run slowly on their own into a siding ahead, their movement controlled by a shunter or porter running alongside and applying the brakes on one of the wagons. *Fly shunting* was different in that the locomotive was *ahead* of the wagons, i.e. between them and their intended destination. What happened was the engine gave a pull to get them on the move, the vehicles were deftly uncoupled and the engine dashed ahead on to one line, the points were changed and the wagons were diverted on to another. Usually it worked!

In 1914 the staff at Morpeth Goods Station was as shown in the accompanying diagram.

The traffic foreman would be on duty from 6.00 am until 5.30 pm; his assistant from 10.30 am until 10.00 pm, meal times included. The first shift of shunters and yard porters began work at 5.30 am and finished at 5.00 pm: the second shift was from 4.00 pm until about 2.00 am the following morning. The checkers and gangs would be there either from 6.00 am to 5.30 pm or from 8.30 am to 8.00 pm, often later. The carts for delivering or collecting goods were known as *rulleys*. The first rulleyman would normally start at 6.30 am, to be followed

by the second man an hour later. No journey from the yard was made
after 5.00 pm though, of course, some traders brought in their own
after that. The six clerks covered such duties as the collection of
accounts in the town and the inspection of and reporting on claims
for damage; correspondence arising out of received traffic; invoicing
and correspondence relating to forward traffic; abstraction of in-
voices and the preparation of weekly statements; compilation of
delivery sheets for rulleymen, the keeping of the register of wagons,
and the making of returns to the Railway Clearing House; the advising
of customers of the arrival of goods, plus various miscellaneous
duties. The job of the checker was to see that, in the case of forward
traffic for example, the goods corresponded with the declaration on
the consignment note, and that everything was weighed and securely
packed. He then marked on the consignment note the route and the
number of the wagon into which the items had to be loaded. The
porters were there to move the various articles where required. The
loaders were responsible for loading wagons safely and carefully to
prevent damage in transit and in such a way that they could be
unloaded easily.

   Before considering specific merchandise on the Blyth & Tyne
Branch it is relevant to include at this stage the main goods stations
at Newcastle namely Trafalgar, The Forth and New Bridge Street. The
huge depot at Trafalgar, built originally in the early 1850s by the York,
Newcastle & Berwick Railway, became a full load and storage depot
after 1871. It was closed in January 1907 and demolished to make
room for the lines between New Bridge Street station and Manors.
The Forth, opened in March 1871, became the centre for all
consignments to and from the Blyth & Tyne after December 1874. All
Newcastle city traffic was handled there though after 1895 tranships
were transferred to the major centre at Gateshead. New Bridge Street
Goods, designed by William Bell, was one of the first reinforced
concrete structures in the country. Situated alongside the line
between Manors and Jesmond, it was partly opened in January 1907
and completely in use in 1912. Originally there were four floors with
wagon hoists, plus a cellar area which accommodated 40 wagons.
The upper floors were used for storing bulk materials. The yard could
accommodate over 300 wagons. There were five cart roads between
tracks, plus a loading dock, and six tracks with four benches under
cover. Newcastle escaped relatively lightly during the war but this
goods station was largely devastated by several incendiary bombs

STAFF AT MORPETH GOODS STATION c1914

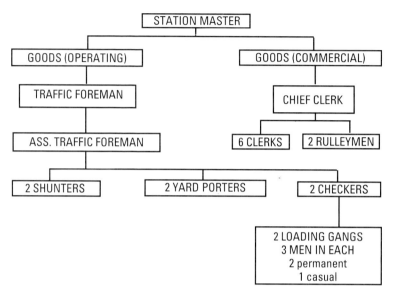

and burned for weeks afterwards. The night it was hit, in September 1941, the glow in the sky could be seen thirty-five miles away. Later the wrecked upper parts of the building were demolished but it continued to handle the fruit and vegetables for Newcastle Green Market. Train loads of banana vans could often be seen, steam heated from the engine to help ripen the fruit during transit.

By contrast, the tiny goods station at Holywell was mainly concerned with loads from a local brickyard. For several years from about the mid 1940s two former North Eastern vans (one a 15-ton Road van) parked at the buffers of the single siding were used to store Silcock's animal foods prior to delivery to farms. At Hepscott, near Morpeth, the warehouse was a small wooden structure 12 ft long and 10 ft wide which stood on the platform.

The goods shed and warehouse at Blyth was of an early NER pattern and style capable of holding six wagons. It was 140 ft long and 42 ft wide with three loading bays for road traffic and two 1½ ton cranes. It was extended by an open dock 33 ft in length. The goods yard area could hold well over 100 wagons. There were a long side dock and an end dock, together with a 10-ton crane, all used for loading and unloading. To understand the significance of the railway at Blyth over the years it is necessary to look at the port and some of the industries round about.

In the Clerk's half-yearly Report to Blyth Harbour Commissioners, of December 1909, it was stated that Pyman, Bell & Company had agreed to import 20,000 - 30,000 loads of timber at Blyth. Figures for that year and the previous one were given thus:-

	1908	1909
FOR MINING	2,476 loads	7,143 loads
OTHER SAWN TIMBER	5,129 loads	6,607 loads

It was reported that Blyth was becoming known as a good harbour for herring boats. It was anticipated this business would greatly increase the following year, meanwhile details were given as shown:-

ARRIVALS AT BLYTH: FISHING BOATS

	1908	1909
Steamers with fish	162	1648
Sailing boats with fish	86	498
Vessels fishing from the port:		
Steamers	91	333
Sailing boats	79	214

In 1912 The Port of Blyth Fishing Co was started but with the outbreak of war vessels were taken over by the Government, fish curers' sheds and plots were requisitioned, the ice factory was dismantled and machinery was sold. The fishing industry at Blyth never recovered. During the First World War a submarine base was established there.

Blyth was a very active shipbuilding and ship repair centre with some noteworthy constructions to its credit including the first Ark Royal. The well-known firm of shipbreakers, Hughes Bolckow, had a large yard on the north side of the river with a rail connection. "Britannia", the largest 3-decker sailing ship ever built (the keel for which was laid at Portsmouth in 1860) was eventually broken up at Blyth in 1916. The 12,350-ton battleship "Renown" (1914), submarines, tankers, cargo vessels and ships of all kinds from various countries were stripped and taken apart. In one ten-year period the firm dismantled over 70 ships. One sideline was the making of teak furniture from ships' timbers including a set of seats for the terraces at the House of Commons. Seats from Blyth were sent to several American Universities and to a number of countries.

These industries, together with several smaller concerns and general town trade, brought considerable amounts of forwarded and received traffic to Blyth over the years. The first fish train ran on 27 July 1910, hauled by engine no. 1745. Pit props, used to support the roof in colliery workings, were regular loads at one time. Materials for the submarines included ammunition, while for the shipyards all kinds of steel sheet, rudders, engines and propellers were received. During World War II army lorries were carried into and out of the town by rail. In 1955 forwardings included 15,000 tons of timber, 37,732 tons of scrap metal and 617 tons of manganese. Traffic received that year included 6,500 tons of timber, 1,283 tons of steel for the National Coal Board, 4,621 tons of iron and steel for Blyth Dry Docks, 659 tons of pipes and 1,227 tons of bricks for the Northern Gas Board. Nearly 9,000 tons of steel were also received for the new power station at Cambois (pronounced Camus) near North Blyth. Figures given below show details for 1962:-

Goods traffic carted*	4,017 tons	(*i.e. delivered)
Parcels traffic carted	1,739 tons	
Parcels traffic carted by hired vehicles	226 tons	
Coal traffic dealt with in private sidings	36,276 tons	(Northern Gas Board)
Coal traffic dealt with in goods yard	700 tons	(other merchants)

At Tynemouth, the former NER terminus was used largely for coal after the new station was built in 1882. The old station area of the former Blyth & Tyne Railway at North Shields Terminus, near the Master Mariners' Homes, was used for goods traffic and a connection was made round a tight curve at the south end of the new station. Fish trains were usually loaded in one of the bay platforms. Once on the main line and running at express speeds these trains could be unloaded in London twelve hours later. In its day Tynemouth handled general supplies for the shops and private premises up to Whitley Bay and Monkseaton, container traffic for factories, sweets from a local producer, building materials and manure. Tanks and other army vehicles have been received for the Teritorial Centre built on the site of the Blyth & Tyne terminus.

On the Branch in general could be seen loads of bricks, straw or hay, farm implements, sacks of grain, sand for use on locomotives, engine boilers, material for collieries, cement and oil - to name a few.

Yards and sidings were provided with a loading gauge under which
high-loaded wagons were tested to make sure they would pass safely
under bridges and through tunnels.

The North Eastern Railway had a good fleet of general purpose
wagons and vans, plus special vehicles, many of which continued in
use through LNER days, some even into British Railways. LNER
wagons were painted in a basic colour scheme of grey for *unfitted*
stock - that is with brakes not operated from the engine, red-oxide
for vehicles whose brakes could be worked from the engine, white
for refrigerated vans and some fish vans. Fully braked goods trains
could travel at much higher speeds but there was an advantage in
having some trains partly *fitted* with continuous brakes. Even six
wagons next to the locomotive gave extra braking power to the train.
An LNER wagon carried the letters NE on its sides, also its number,
the load the wagon could carry, its tare weight, and a code name if
applicable. Sometimes special instructions were given such as NOT
TO BE LOOSE SHUNTED. Somewhere on the underframe would be
a plate showing its number, where built, when and by whom. The
codes would sometimes give an indication of the type of wagon, for
example:-

LOWMAC   low wagon for machinery
BOGIE BOLSTER   a long, low, bogie wagon fitted with bolsters
TUBE   open wagon suitable for long pipes, etc.
CONFLAT   flat wagon for container traffic
TRESTLE   a wagon fitted to carry steel plates at an angle.

Sometimes letters were added to the code to denote different
lengths of wagon, or carrying capacity. Codes were carried forward
into British Railways with some modifications.

At places where rolling stock gathered, in larger goods yards and
near staiths, wagon examiners and fitters were employed to maintain
the wagons. Oiling of bearings was most important to ensure they did
not 'run hot'. Wheels could be changed but vehicles requiring more
serious repairs were sent to Walkergate Carriage & Wagon Works at
Heaton. Any wagon not fit to run was known as a *cripple*. If, after
minor repairs it would still not be able to travel on its own wheels it
was loaded on to a suitable truck and sent to the Works.

On a local line, freight was usually moved by pick-up goods trains
which attached and detached wagons at the various stations, though
where there was sufficient traffic a train may be timetabled for fewer
stops or to work straight through to its desination. Railwaymen -

certainly in the Newcastle area - referred to a branch goods train as *the pilot*. On the Blyth & Tyne Branch pilots were scheduled from Blyth, Percy Main and Heaton at various times and a North Blyth engine was used to work goods and cattle over the Wansbeck Valley line from Morpeth. Wagons for or from Blyth & Tyne stations were sorted in Heaton Marshalling Yard.

An entry in a signal box Occurrence Book on 29 December 1908 read:-

"On taking duty at 1.00 pm line blocked between Woodhorn and Newbiggin. Engine 229 Pilot Goods fast *(i.e. stuck)* in snow drift. Snowplough arrived 2.24 left at 2.29 pm and line clear again about 4.00 pm. Heavy detention to traffic by same, also Points and Signals working very irregularly.

T. Swan on duty."

In the mid 1950s coal from the Bedlington area intended for local agents was first taken to Seghill. At night it was moved on to New Bridge Street Coal Depot for merchants who were based there, but any wagon loads for Benton, South Gosforth and West Jesmond were shunted off at Benton. A pick-up goods from Heaton which followed, running via the south west curve, shunted the small yard at Benton leaving such commodities as basic slag and bricks, then took forward the coal and any goods for South Gosforth and West Jesmond. This pilot also left empty vans at the Lucozade factory between Longbenton and South Gosforth and collected loaded ones. Benton and South Gosforth were two stations where the coal sale was in charge of the Station Master, a system introduced by the NER as a perk but which continued in LNER and BR days.

A contrast to pick-up goods trains over part of the Blyth & Tyne route was a fully-fitted express freight which in the 1940s travelled each weekday from New Bridge Street to Benton, where it joined the main line via the north west curve. Known as 'the Niddrie goods', it conveyed 40-50 loads of empty beer barrels in open wagons and some converted cattle trucks (designated ALE wagons) to Edinburgh. The engine was invariably a War Department type, usually a 2-8-0 but occasionally a 2-10-0. Any other freight trains using the north west curve were irregular diversions during track repairs or minor derailments.

Inevitably, with strong competition from road haulage, more and more merchandise was taken from the railways and it becomes totally uneconomic to run partly filled wagons to places all over the country.

The way ahead for the railways was to concentrate on block loads, particularly for long hauls for which they were ideally suited. Under modernisation schemes, small capacity wagons were gradually phased out and the vehicles built for particular cargoes were also withdrawn. By 1964 the number of freight wagons on British Railways had been reduced to 722,166. New modern rolling stock was introduced and firms were encouraged either to rent wagons or to run train loads of their own behind BR locomotives.

The Blyth & Tyne Branch served the needs of so many communities over numerous years but goods traffic was withdrawn from its stations between 1963 and 1967 apart from Monkseaton and Tynemouth (1959). Nevertheless, in the autumn of 1968 construction started at Lynemouth, near Ashington, of a large aluminium smelter for Alcan UK Ltd. Limited production commenced in March 1972 and was gradually increased. Eight miles away, on the north bank of the River Blyth storage silos for imported alumina (15,000 tons capacity) and calcined petroleum coke (7,500 tons capacity) were built. These raw materials were transported by rail between Cambois and Lynemouth. A line from Ashington to Lynemouth was used for the purpose of conveying trains to and from the works.

Short trains of fuel oil were taken to the diesel depot at Cambois but this was not a revenue-earning service and it was eventually transferred to road.

It is worth reporting that, thanks to modern technology, the location, load, destination and several other details of any wagon can now be obtained by computer simply by feeding in its number. If it is in transit the estimated time of arrival is also shown - a far cry from the army of number-takers whose efforts used to help the railways keep records of wagon movements.

```
NEWSHAM GOODS TRAFFIC
NEWSHAM GOODS TRAFFIC 1962
FORWARDED
    Merchandise                  32 wagon loads : 282 tons
    Minerals, excluding coal      3 wagon loads : 33 tons
RECEIVED
    Coal                      2,926 wagon loads : 50,330 tons
    Minerals (blue stone for
    barging out to sea)       1,367 wagon loads : 26,098 tons
    Merchandise                 393 wagon loads : 2,383 tons
BEBSIDE OPENCAST COAL 1962
    35,680 wagon loads forwarded  (estimated 749,280 tons)
```

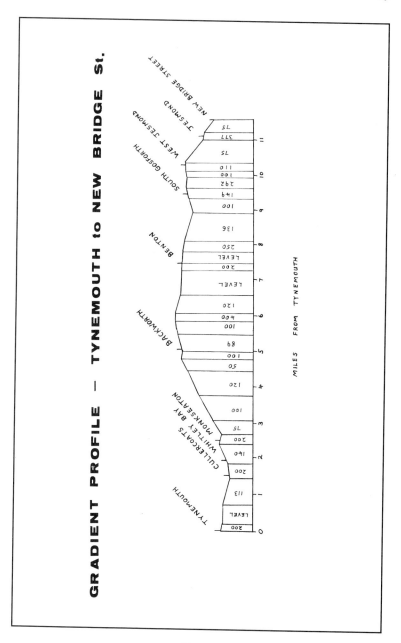

Fig. 13

Chapter 9

Motive Power Depots

THE PURPOSE OF a motive power depot is to provide reliable locomotives to haul different kinds of train, bearing in mind such things as loads to be moved, speed required, distance and the specified route. Various types of locomotive were allocated to depots to cover these requirements but how long they stayed depended on circumstances such as their age, a change in traffic, the introduction of more modern/powerful motive power, major overhaul at the Works, or pressing needs elsewhere. Some were based at the same shed for many years but as they became superseded were relegated to less demanding duties.

When a locomotive finished its shift certain essential tasks had to be performed. The tender (or bunker if it was a tank engine) was filled with coal and the water tank replenished. The fire was cleaned out and ash and clinker removed. Much of this at one time was taken away to be used as ballast for the track. If the loco was not required for some time the fire was drawn, then relit when needed to raise steam. Ash, soot and grit which collected at the front of the engine had to be removed regularly so that it would give its best performance. Routine inspections and maintenance were carried out and any faults reported by a driver would be rectified.

Most people are familiar with the pictures which show an engine crew on the Liverpool & Manchester Railway in top hat and tails. No doubt this was for a special occasion but it does underline the status of an engine driver. In the days when railways were at their zenith, in the 1880s for example, North Eastern Railway drivers were paid 7s 6d (37$\frac{1}{2}$p) per day which was good money in those days. Nevertheless, the aspirations of many had to be tempered with patience as it took several years to become a driver, more for a top-link man. The appearance of a locomotive was considered by management to be very important. If it was well painted in a distinctive livery and kept clean (even a goods engine) it was a good advertisement for the Company, and this is where it all began - anyone who wanted to drive an engine had to start by being a cleaner. His work took him all over and under the engines so that he learnt quite a lot about them, which, together with listening to and joining in everyday chat, and studying, would give him a good background knowledge. A cleaner with reasonable service and conduct who passed his examination was known as a *passed cleaner.* He could then be available to fill in as a temporary fireman on shed or shunting duties and eventually would be promoted to that rank.

As a fireman he would at first be confined to shunting duties around goods yards, stations, depots or staiths. He would learn such things as how to handle the shovel, how to feed coal accurately into the firebox, the response of the locomotive to the regulator or brake, when to use the injector, how to couple up and, very importantly, how to carry out his duties orderly and methodically. He would become familiar with track and point formations, various signals, whistle codes, hand signals, railway expressions - and would learn how to work with others as a team. After a thorough grounding he would be allowed on trips away from the depot, then slowly and gradually work his way through the 'links', all the time absorbing information about signals, locations, gradients and other essentials about particular routes. With practice he should be able to tell where he was in the dark by the multitude of sounds. By experience, reading, listening to others, attending classes and passing stringent examinations he would become a *passed fireman* and be available for relief driver's duties at the bottom end of the scale.

If his service and reliability warranted it a man would become a driver, starting on shunting duties as before. Not every depot however, provided engines and men for the most important trains, the province of top-link men.

At the beginning of a shift a driver and his fireman reported for duty. The driver might be given a booklet of special notices relating to the area in which he was to work. This would contain information such as track repairs, speed restrictions, diversions, extra trains, retimings, water columns not working, anything that was not routine and which the driver should know. He would then examine the notice board (sometimes called *the dockie)* which would show his engine for the day, where it was standing and its specific duties. The driver then had up to an hour to prepare his engine, checking coal, water, sand boxes, and making sure all moving parts were well oiled. Meanwhile from the stores the fireman drew loco lamps, tools and a bucket together with emergency flags and detonators. A detonator is an explosive about the size of the yolk of a fried egg which was clipped to lines as a warning to other trains in the event of an accident or derailment. They were also used during fog when they were placed singly on the line at a distant signal if it was showing caution. A driver, hearing one of these explode under his wheels, would then expect to find the next home signal at danger. These were used long before automatic warning systems were introduced.

A driver needed a thorough knowledge of his engine and had to know its power and capabilities. It is a well known fact nonetheless that each steam locomotive had a 'character' of its own: even those of the same type built at the same works within days of one another would never perform identically. Some steamed freely, others badly; some rode well, others were rough; some were prone to slip, others hardly ever . . .

The Blyth & Tyne Branch had three essential sub-sheds namely North Blyth, South Blyth and Percy Main. When the North Eastern Railway absorbed the Blyth & Tyne Railway in 1874 Percy Main was the centre for building and repairing locomotives and rolling stock. The buildings consisted of a running shed, repair shops and separate shops for carriages and wagons. The NER did not require these facilities as they duplicated in some degree what was available elsewhere in the area. The running shed was made into a three road through shed whereas the former repair shop was converted into a 'dead-end' shed with five tracks. Part of this was destroyed by fire early in 1921 but was rebuilt. In the early 1900s the old wagon shop was demolished to make room for a turntable. Up to c.1920 Percy Main was one of the major centres of the NER for cutting up redundant locomotives of all classes.

Because of the vast amount of coal traffic it was necessary to have a shed on both sides of the River Blyth. If there had been only one it would have meant an excessive amount of light engine movements as traffic built up. The building of a depot at South Blyth to accommodate nine locomotives was completed in 1879 but in 1895 the capacity was doubled to make a six-road run-in (or dead-end) shed. North Blyth was opened in 1897 but the design there was of a central turntable with 22 radiating stalls to hold one tender engine each, in a rectangular building. From the days of the North Eastern Railway, through the LNER era and into British Railways these three sheds handled the bulk of the coal produced in the area though, naturally, locos from other depots also worked on the Blyth & Tyne Branch.

To handle its Tynemouth trains the Blyth & Tyne Railway had built a small two-lane shed at the north west side of New Bridge Street station. This was demolished by the NER about 1902 so that the

Framed by an NER footbridge at Beamish Museum these two locomotives show different designs of 0-6-0 locomotives. On the left is an industrial saddle tank with outside cylinders. The class C tender engine on the right is NER number 876. (David A Wells, LBIPP)

connecting line to Manors could be put in. To replace this, a new shed, 150 feet long with two roads, was built at South Gosforth but it was only used for two or three years.

There are various ways of identifying steam locomotives of which the main ones are by number, wheel arrangement and class. Power from the cylinders (which may be on the outside of the locomotive, on the inside, or both) is transmitted by cranks to the *driving wheels*. These are usually coupled by stout rods to others of the same diameter. To help spread the weight of the engine there may be smaller, supporting wheels ahead of or behind the driving wheels, or both. These are known as *leading wheels* and *trailing wheels*. Under the Whyte system, an engine with six driving wheels (counting both sides) coupled together but no leading or trailing wheels is known as an 0-6-0; one with four driving wheels, no leading wheels, and four trailing wheels is an 0-4-4. The letter T after a wheel arrangement denotes a tank engine - that is it does not have a separate tender for carrying coal and water and the water tanks are alongside the boiler. ST stands for *saddle tank* where the water tank straddles the boiler; and WT (when used) indicates a *well tank* where the water carrier is concealed below the engine under the coal bunker. The diagram on page 95 shows some of the different wheel arrangements.

All locomotives carried a number on the cab sides, tank sides or tender (often, too, on the front buffer beam) as a means of identification. It should be remembered, however, that not only were numbers changed on occasions but wholesale renumbering took place from time to time hence caution is needed when using a number alone to classify a certain engine. The NER also used to renumber surplus engines which were withdrawn but retained in reserve. This was known as the Duplicate List and occasionally certain engines could carry the same number.

Recognition by class is a well used method though there can be complications there, too. The North Eastern's system was to use letters and numbers or numbers only as a way of putting their locomotives into convenient groups.

A system was introduced by the LNER in which the wheel arrangement was indicated by a specific letter. All 4-6-2s were class A, for instance; 0-6-0s were J and 2-6-2 types were V. This was followed by a number to designate the particular type and sometimes there was a second number separated by an oblique to portray a difference in detail, say, some modification, or a re-build.

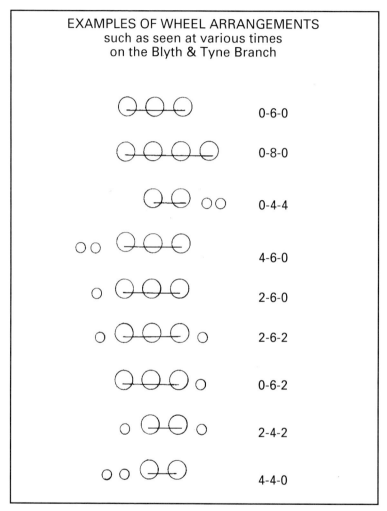

EXAMPLES OF WHEEL ARRANGEMENTS
such as seen at various times
on the Blyth & Tyne Branch

0-6-0

0-8-0

0-4-4

4-6-0

2-6-0

2-6-2

0-6-2

2-4-2

4-4-0

Fig. 14

In LNER days, too, the shed at which a loco was based was painted on the front buffer beam as was the class to which it belonged. Later, under British Railways, the shed was represented by a code on a small, oval plate on the smokebox door. Percy Main became 52E from 1949 and both Blyth sheds were 52F even though they were totally independent. An 'A' suffix signified the parent, or area, shed in this case Gateshead, 52A. British Railways also introduced a power classification rated from 1 to 9 for passenger, freight and mixed traffic engines, shown as 7P, 5F, 4MT, etc. In BR days engines carried a Route Availability (RA) code usually on the cab sides, again from 1 to 9. All routes and places where engines would work were given a classification under the same system and only locos up to the same category could be used on them. Factors taken into account included weight and length of engine, overhang on curves, severity of curves, platform and bridge clearances and the standard of track. The Blyth & Tyne Branch running lines were all RA9 consequently all locomotives, even express passenger types, could be used. For obvious reasons engines working on staiths were restricted to small shunting types, RA2.

The North Eastern Railway was fortunate in having Locomotive Superintendents who produced aesthetic designs for efficient, spirited and reliable locomotives, far ahead of rival companies. It is appropriate to consider some of these which worked tirelessly on the Branch, before taking a general look at the motive power. One of the most successful 0-6-0s was the class C introduced in 1886 by T W Worsdell. Most of these were originally *compounds* in which the steam was used twice, first in the high pressure 18" cylinder then in the low pressure 26" diameter cylinder. This idea was complicated and expensive in terms of maintenance so Wilson Worsdell, who succeeded his brother, converted the whole class to *simple* engines in which both cylinders were 18" in diameter and the steam was used once only. They became class C1 and many were fitted with brakes which enabled them to work passenger trains. The last of this type of 201 engines (LNER J21) survived until 1961 but in their day they could manage 40-50 wagons in fast goods trains on the main line.

The first 3-cylinder design attributed to (Sir) Vincent Raven was a sturdy and powerful 4-6-2T, primarily for short distance runs with mineral trains. Fitted with automatic brakes, they were used for a time on the sets of 40-ton coal wagons between Ashington and Blyth. Twenty were built of which several were placed at Blyth, where they were found to be good performers. They were capable of hauling 1,000 ton loads on the level at 20 mph. One of these Class Ys on test lifted 850 tons on a rising gradient of 1:150 and accelerated the train to 10 mph in half a mile (C J Allen, 'The North Eastern Railway'). On one occasion a class Y on an unfitted coal train was unable to hold its load down Benton south east curve but this was probably driver error.

NER Class C locomotives (LNER/BR J21), designed by T. W. Worsdell, were introduced in 1886. Four remained in use in 1960 but were withdrawn shortly afterwards. 65033 is shown at South Blyth. (J A Wells)

J27 number 65874 outside the shed at South Blyth. (J A Wells)

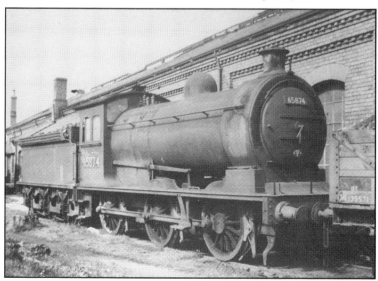

One of the unsung mainstays of local passenger traffic all over the
NER area was the smart class 0 0-4-4 tanks (LNER G5) first introduced
in 1894. They were even used to run some of the Newcastle to
Middlesbrough expresses and certainly performed with gusto. Almost all of the 110 locos in this class passed into BR ownership and
it was at the end of 1958 that the last four were withdrawn from South
Blyth, having been replaced by the infiltration of diesel multiple units.

Without doubt the real Trojans of the Blyth & Tyne Branch were the
P3s (LNER J27) - tough 0-6-0s with a capacity for hard work. They had
a boiler diameter of 5 ft 6 ins which gave them a very robust
appearance.

Introduced in 1906 and produced until 1923, some of these fine
machines put in over sixty year's service hauling millions of tons of
coal. Even more invincible were the Raven T2 0-8-0s, which had
prodigious hauling power and were unsurpassed when they first
appeared in 1913. Forerunners of this class were the Ts and T1s. The
class T locomotives were designed to move loads of 60 full wagons
though they could manage twelve more than that without difficulty,
making 1,170 tons without the brake van. 'The Engineer' in 1901
recorded a train of 1,326¹/₄ tons, 569 yards in length, being moved by
a 'T' at Tyne Dock, "the longest loaded train with which the Company
had ever dealt." It covered 11 miles in 52 minutes. Similar trials were
carried out at Blyth in July 1903 with engine number 651 which was
built the previous month. Fifty of the T1s were sent to France in the
First World War and when they returned to the North East they carried
three inverted stripes and an exploding bomb emblem on their front
sandboxes to mark their service with the Army. Some of these were
to be seen on the Branch afterwards.

As mentioned elsewhere, Occurrence Books in signal boxes gave
information about events which may have caused delay to traffic. The
details opposite are representative summaries of entries in three such
books from the Ashington area. In each case the locomotive number
was recorded but these have been supplemented courtesy of Mr J M
Fleming who traced the class and the year built.

Although North Blyth was predominantly a mineral shed, at the end
of NER days there were three passenger turns, two between
Bedlington and Newbiggin and one from Manors North to Morpeth,
covered by BTP tanks and 2-4-2 tanks. The LNER continued to use
the South Blyth G5 0-4-4 tanks for loco-hauled passenger trains on
the Branch. For many years, including BR days, two trains in each

DATE	LOCO.	REASON FOR ENTRY	CLASS	BUILT
18 Feb. 1898	1932	Took first set of coal from Woodhorn Colliery	P1	Dec. 1897
17 Mar. 1898	797 ⎫ 1435 ⎭	Unable to take load of 22 wagons from colliery Assisted to advance signal by 1435	398 BTP	Dec. 1872 Oct. 1875
19 Aug. 1902	1961	5 wagons derailed entering Linton branch	P1	May 1898
8 June 1903	897	Took wrong line - points wedged with stone	398	Nov. 1874
13 June 1903	1694	Broken coupling hook	T	Feb. 1903
15 Nov. 1905	387	Derailed one pair driving wheels. Re-railed himself and departed with theatrical special to Bedlington	O	Sept 1901
2 Sept. 1906	1919	Engine detaching carriage truck mounted rail on crossing and was derailed	O	June 1897
29 Apr. 1908	594	On goods. Damaged points : signalman's error	603	Nov 1879
29 Dec. 1908	229	Goods pilot stuck in snowdrift between Woodhorn and Newbiggin. Dug out by snowploughs	36	Dec. 1880
24 Jan. 1911	1186	On empties. Signal stuck. Driver told to pass it at danger	T	May 1903
2 May 1911	1129	Damaged points when coming out of colliery	Y	Dec. 1910
25 May 1912	839	Misunderstanding over signal	P3	May 1906
26 June 1912	1439	Broken rail	290	Formerly a BTP, rebuilt July 1901
28 Apr. 1913	952	Engine failure. Placed in siding by relief engine from Bedlington (number not shown).	BTP	May 1874
	1964	Took 952 to North Blyth	P1	June 1899
13 Feb. 1915	1940	Engine shunting when points failed causing delay to 12.50 p.m. passenger train at Woodhorn	P	Dec. 1891
29 July 1915	1997	Stopped for wagon brake to be released	P1	Apr. 1899
17 Feb. 1916	133	Last engine cautioned after wire down	C	Dec. 1899
18 July 1916	1961 ⎫ 1183 ⎭	"As goods engine No. 1961 was pushing into goods yard from Up line, engine burst a tube. Phoned No. Blyth and (was) instructed to put 1183 standing here to goods and send 1961 home. Driver refused and left 2.38 p.m. taking 1961 with him to No. Blyth."	P1 Y	May 1899 Mar. 1911
12 Jan. 1917	871	Woodhorn to New Bridge St. coal. Guard reported 20-ton loaded wagon derailed in colliery	C	Mar. 1899

Fig. 15. Specific locomotives mentioned in Occurrence Books

direction between Newcastle or Manors and Newbiggin were run by
V1 or V3 2-6-2T engines from Heaton shed. These were nicknamed
Teddy Bears by local railwaymen. On rare occasions the Heaton turns
were covered by engines of class B1, D20, D49, J21, J25, J39, K1, K3
and L1 - even an odd A3 on a running-in duty. Coal and goods
continued to be worked mainly by J21, J24, J25, J27, Q5 and Q6
engines, while for shunting there were J72 and J77 tank engines. The
stalwarts of the North Eastern Railway, which had served the LNER
so well during the twenty-five years of its existence, continued to be
the principal motive power in the reign of British Railways. After the
change of ownership in January 1948 all LNER locomotives had
60,000 added to their number.

All North Eastern Railway engines were basically green in colour
with red buffer beams, and lined out, though there were variations
between the different Works - Gateshead, Darlington and York. From
1904 NER goods engines appeared in black livery with some lining.
Both the LNER and BR favoured black for their goods and local
passenger engines.

J27 locomotives continued to outnumber all other types at Blyth. At
Percy Main also their entire fleet of 24 engines in 1950, and 21 in 1959,
were of this class. On a branch such as the Blyth & Tyne some regular
runs were scheduled but many crews worked on Control Orders
which meant they completed one trip then were informed verbally
where they had to go next. A typical shift with a J27, 5F, is given
below: This was compiled from a guard's journal about the mid
1950s:-

Leaving the shed at 6.15 am the engine proceeded to the van line
where it attached brake van number 730940. The engine and van
went to the nearby mineral sidings and from there took 33 empty coal
wagons to Lynemouth Colliery, beyond Ashington. The 'empties'
were shunted off and 21 loaded wagons were picked up which were
taken back to North Blyth and left in reception sidings ready to be
pushed on to the staiths. Another load of 25 empties was hooked on
and the engine took water before running this train to a colliery at
Bedlington, where the wagons were detached. The engine and van
had then to go along the Morpeth branch to Choppington colliery for
22 loaded wagons for North Blyth. This meant *running round* at
Bedlington and placing the brake van on the other end of the train
before continuing down the other side of the junction. 65893 spent
a short time taking water and followed this by shunting in the sidings

at North Blyth for almost an hour, sorting wagons and making up empty sets for different collieries. The next duty was another trip to Lynemouth with 32 empties, returning with a full load of 22 wagons. These were shunted off in the sidings prior to being teemed into waiting ships. As this was the end of the shift the brake van was left in the van line and the engine returned to the shed for coal, water and fire cleaning at 2.40 pm. Within a few hours '58-93' would be back 'on the road' with a different crew.

A bonus was payable if work was completed in an allotted time though this was not a new idea. A document dated 1932, set out in detail a Scheme of Special Payments Applicable to Trainmen Working Mineral Trains from North & South Blyth. Pages of running times between various places were given, of which these are an extract:-

NORTH BLYTH TO:-	WINTER Loaded mins.	Engine & Van mins.	SUMMER Loaded mins.	Engine & Van mins
Bedlington Station	42	33	40	29
Bedlington E	30	23	24	23
Bedlington F	24	17	24	14
Cambois	17	17	14	11
West Blyth	13	11	12	10
North Blyth Van Line	—	5	—	5
Ashington Colliery	32	23	31	19
Linton	46	33	43	27
Ellington	47	34	45	28
Woodhorn	36	26	34	21
Newbiggin Colliery	42	30	42	26
Ashington Station	27	19	27	16
North Seaton	36	26	32	24
Newbiggin Station	37	27	33	25
Lynemouth	57	40	55	34

7 minutes were allowed on each occasion it was required for the engine to take water, though if it was necessary for the engine to go to Alnmouth from Shilbottle to turn no allowance was made for that. On 17 December 1959 steam locomotives at South Blyth were shown as follows:-

J21   0-6-0   2F   65070
J25   0-6-0   3F   65663 65727
(65706 was withdrawn on 7 Dec.)

J27   0-6-0   5F   65799 65800 65810   65815 65822
                     65834 65838 65861   65862 65877
                     65891.
                     65808 was receiving boiler repairs.
                     *65824 and 65847 were not available
                          for work owing to collision
                          damage.

J77   0-6-0T 2F   68408
                     *These locomotives were involved in an accident at
                     West Sleekburn on 4 November 1959 between two
                     mineral trains. (See page 132)

By 1965 some K1 2-6-0s and more Q6s had been drafted into Blyth
Sheds. Percy Main shed was closed to steam in February 1965 when
its remaining J27s were sent to Sunderland (1), North Blyth (3) and
South Blyth (10). For another year over thirty diesel shunters were
shedded there then transferred to Gateshead.

At Blyth, the J27s, sadly, were withdrawn shortly before the end of
steam on the Branch and their clean-cut lines were replaced by
grotesque 4MT 2-6-0s from the Midland Region. South Blyth was
closed to steam on 28 May 1967 and its remaining five J27s were
passed over to Sunderland to end their days. Diesels remained at the
depot until 29 January 1968 when Cambois was opened. The North
shed survived until 9 September 1967, just a few days before steam
was withdrawn altogether from the area. The five remaining 'foreign'
engines went for scrap.

Readers may be interested to know some details of three vehicles
at North Blyth in August 1967 which had been used as storage areas.
One was a Gresley full brake built in 1938, lettered "Storage Van CM
& EE's Department NE Region". Its number was shown as DE 321097
but stencilled on the solebar was "Vehicle No. E70528E." The second
one, formerly an LMS gunpowder van with a tare weight of 7-17, was
numbered MO42266. The builder's plate showed "LMS Standard
287784, Carlestown 1929." The original cast notice on the right hand
door stated "No unauthorised person to open these doors". Thirdly,
there was the grounded body of an outside framed van on which
could just be detected "NE 620133 10 tons."

Locomotives of various classes, probably including some from
Blyth, were cut up at Hughes Bolckow's yard, and an Ashington firm
rented a siding at Choppington for the same purpose.

With so much combustible material lying around and sparks from hot ashes flying about, motive power depots were without doubt fire hazards. What is not widely known is that sheds and works had their own fire-fighting teams. The LNER's General Rules & Regulations for Fire Brigades 1925 edition will serve as an example. The number of 'fire-men' (or fire fighters) at North and South Blyth, including officers, was 12 each but there was no fire engine at either depot. Percy Main shed had 10 firemen and there was a manual engine - unlike Gateshead Locomotive Works which had a steam engine mounted on a truck.

Officers in charge of Fire Brigades were appointed by the Divisional Firemaster and were held responsible for the efficiency of the men and for the fire appliances connected with their Brigades. Their duties included the examination of all fire appliances on the first Friday of each month - with the inevitable report on the appropriate forms to the District Firemaster; arranging regular practices to ensure each man attended the minimum number of drills; keeping up to date lists of firemen, and giving instructions in the use of hydrants and how to attack different kinds of fire. Firemen were required to attend a minimum of six drills a year and, among other things, had to report for duty at the outbreak of a fire.

Rates of pay were:-

	Captains	Lieutenants	Engineers	Firemen	
Retaining fees per year	20/-	15/-	12/-	10/-	
Drills, within ordinary hours	1/-	1/-	1/-	1/-	per drill
Drills, outside ordinary hours	2/-	2/-	2/-	2/-	per drill
Attendance at fires within ordinary hours	4/-	3/-	2/-	2/-	first hour
	3/-	2/-	1/-	1/-	per hour after first hour
outside ordinary hours	5/-	4/-	3/-	3/-	first hour
	4/-	3/-	2/-	2/-	per hour after first hour

Fees paid for drills and attendance were in addition to ordinary wages.

Rule 14 of the Rules and Regulations stated "In an emergency, a truck sheet or tarpaulin may be made to serve as a jumping sheet, with as much hay, straw or similar material as can be quickly gathered together, strewn underneath. Should a sheet not be available the hay or straw alone will, of course, help to break a person's fall."

Cambois Depot, situated about one and a half miles from North Blyth was opened at the end of January 1968. Apart from some class 20s in the early days and some class 08 shunters, the diesels there have been 37s and 56s. A few 47s have been used for short periods but are not really suitable for coal haulage out of collieries because of their rapid acceleration. The current situation is included in the final chapter of this book.

DIAGRAM SHOWING NORTH EASTERN RAILWAY LOCOMO-
TIVES MOST FREQUENTLY USED ON THE BLYTH & TYNE
BRANCH AND THEIR LNER CLASSIFICATION

NER CLASS	WHEEL ARRANGEMENT	DESIGNER	FIRST BUILT	LNER CLASS
290	0-6-0T	(see notes below)		J77
398	0-6-0	Edward Fletcher	1872	—
BTP	0-4-4WT	Edward Fletcher	1874	G6
A	2-4-2T	T W Worsdell	1886	F8
C/C1	0-6-0	T W Worsdell	1886	J21
E	0-6-0T	T W Worsdell	1886	J71
E1	0-6-0T	Wilson Worsdell	1898	J72
L	0-6-0T	Wilson Worsdell	1891	J73
O	0-4-4T	Wilson Worsdell	1894	G5
P	0-6-0	Wilson Worsdell	1894	J24
P1	0-6-0	Wilson Worsdell	1898	J25
P2	0-6-0	Wilson Worsdell	1904	J26
P3	0-6-0	Wilson Worsdell	1906	J27
T/T1	0-8-0	Wilson Worsdell	1901	Q5
T2	0-8-0	Vincent Raven	1913	Q6
Y	4-6-2T	Vincent Raven	1910	A7

NOTES

1. 398 CLASS Several passed into LNER ownership but were not given a class.

2. BTP (Bogie Tank Passenger) From 1899 sixty of these

were rebuilt by Wilson Worsdell into 0-6-0 tank engines and became 290 class but forty-six of the original design passed into LNER ownership.

3. As each new design appeared the North Eastern Railway gave it a classification letter in alphabetical sequence. This system was used by T W Worsdell (1885-1890), Wilson Worsdell (1890-1910), and Vincent Raven 1910-1922. Engines built before the T W Worsdell era were given a class *number*, usually corresponding to the first one of the type. The LNER used letters to denote classes by wheel arrange ment - for example all 0-6-0s were J - followed by a number.

Fig. 16

Class 56 number 133 'Crewe Locomotive Works' at Cambois Depot. The black diamonds indicate it is allocated to coal traffic. The grey livery does not enhance these powerful locomotives. (J A Wells)

Chapter 10

Breakdown Trains

TO HELP DEAL WITH derailments and major incidents the North Eastern Railway constructed almost sixty breakdown trains to a standard pattern between 1889 and 1900. These were allocated to most of the large motive power depots, and some smaller ones, with each train covering a radius of up to fifty miles. At first each train consisted of one six-wheeled vehicle for gear, a four-wheeler used as a mess van and for the staff to travel in, plus a crane and a jib wagon. The cranes were operated by hand in the early days, later by steam. As more of the six-wheeled vans were built each train had two of them. One of the last three complete breakdown trains of this style was allocated to Percy Main.

Mess Van number 92187 was of the approved design having coach-type doors which opened outwards. The crew travelled to jobs in this hence seats and tables were included and there were facilities to give the men food and hot drinks during breaks. The two identical six wheeled vans, 92188 and 92189, designated Tool Vans, were slightly over 27 ft in length not including the buffers. They were strongly constructed of wood with horizontal planking, having one sliding door and four, small, recessed windows on each side. There was a footboard running the length of each side, near the wheels, plus a handrail along the body. The roof was fitted with two ventilators. All the vehicles in these trains had screw couplings, locomotive-type buffers and brakes which were operated by the locomotive.

Although both equipment vehicles were called Tool Vans, it was usual for one to carry wood packing. In early days this was known as the Chock Van but it was later termed the Packing Van. The Tool Van proper carried various kinds of hammers, axes, spanners, burners, chains, tackle blocks and lifting jacks. An old, wooden jack, very heavy and standing nearly three feet high, which was found on land near to where the Percy Main engine shed had stood, must have been part of the gear at one time. It was a Haley's Lifting Jack and enquiries to Manchester Library revealed the patent was taken out in 1840 for "an improved lifting jack . . . for raising or removing heavy bodies but also applicable to the packaging or compressing of goods or other substances." It had a lifting capacity of 12 tons. Inside the Tool Van a locker was built into the bodywork at each corner. The door of each one swung outwards and upwards but could be locked with a normal carriage key. It is easy to see why railwaymen in the North East never refer to 'the breakdown train' - it is always *the tool vans!*

In 1922 the Percy Main lifting gear was a 10-ton hand crane built by Cowans Sheldon in 1890, numbered CME8. It later became 901633. The match truck to support the jib, number 641, was renumbered 901692 by the LNER. A 12-ton hand crane, number 11, built at York in 1890 for West Hartlepool, was transferred first to Kirkby Stephen then to Percy Main in 1951, to replace number 8 which was presumably scrapped. Crane number 9, which was based at Tyne Dock in 1922, was at North Blyth in 1966, prior to being withdrawn.

From an analysis of paint, the North Eastern Railway Association ascertained that the Percy Main train had been in crimson lake livery originally. Later repainting by the NER was shown to be bright, red oxide. The LNER renumbered their service vehicles and painted them Oxford blue, an attractive shade but prone to fade quickly. Numbers allocated to the Percy Main trio were:-

Mess Van	(92187)	901610
Packing Van	(92188)	901611
Tool Van	(92189)	901612

For some unknown reason these vans were unique in that 92187 was given its LNER number and painted blue only in 1945, twenty-two years after Grouping! 92188 and 92189, however, retained their North Eastern numbers and livery throughout the period of LNER ownership.

These three vans remained together until about 1960. A letter dated November 1961 sent to depots and signal boxes from the District Operating Superintendent referred to a Combined Tool, Packing and Riding Van number 320740 which had been converted from a vestibuled coach. Instructions were given that this vehicle was not to pass trains on adjacent lines on certain sections at Percy Main, Blyth, Newsham and Bedlington. A similar vehicle, converted from a panelled, Gresley main line coach was stationed at North Blyth in 1967. Built in 1923 it was lettered 'DE 320704 MP E North Blyth', and on an oval plate on the solebar was shown 'NER to carry 8 tons distributed'.

The Tool Van, 92189, was sent to North Blyth where it stood at the end of a siding for use by fitters. It was taken along to Cambois Depot when North Blyth closed. At some time since it left Percy Main a do-it-yourself exercise changed certain details of its appearance. At Cambois it was still used by Carriage & Wagon examiners but it is now at Beamish Museum, near Stanley, County Durham. 92188 spent some years standing at Lynemouth Colliery before being bought by the Tanfield Railway in 1983. There has been some confusion over the identity of these two vehicles for several years but the author was given permission to remove the builder's plate from the vehicle at Cambois and it was definitely 92189. The Riding Van, 92187, was transferred to Tweedmouth from Percy Main where it was used as an office by the Carriage & Wagon Department until that depot closed in 1966. It was probably scrapped after that.

If an accident or derailment on the Blyth & Tyne Branch was too big a job for the Percy Main crane the larger one from Gateshead was called out. To enable breakdown trains from major depots to travel at higher speeds the vans were long, bogied vehicles. In 1960 they consisted of:-

TOOL VAN   DE320135   Built by the Great Northern Railway, date uncertain, as a non-vestibule milk van. The body was 45 feet long and had sliding doors.

TOOL VAN   DE320392   The underframe was constructed in 1935 by the Gloucester Carriage & Wagon Company for a non-vestibule passenger coach. The body was built to the underframe with special arrangements to accommodate power-operated hydraulic jacking equipment carried in the vehicle. As these were of German manufacture the coach was nicknamed the *German Van.*

RIDING VAN DE320700   A Great Northern Railway vehicle built pre-1923 as a brake composite corridor coach with vestibules.

The steam crane was of 45 tons capacity carried on two bogies, with its jib supported on a special wagon. The latter also carried an equalizing beam for use when engines or coaches had overturned or were lying at an angle, plus various wire slings, shackles, blocks and chains. Before any lifting could commence the outriggers had to be in position and 'packed' to prevent the crane from tipping over. Preparation always takes far longer than the actual lift, but once ready an experienced operator can handle a crane with amazing delicacy and accuracy. The Gateshead crane was replaced by one of 75 tons capacity and later still by one powered by a diesel engine. Modern cranes have a two-way radio system between the operator and the chargeman on the job which did away with the old system of giving instructions by various blasts on a whistle.

When the Gateshead Tool Vans visited the Branch the train was drawn by a variety of locomotives - J39, K3, B1, V2, WD 2-8-0 - almost anything that was available at the time.

Although modified and neglected, the distinctive design of the Percy Main tool van number 92189 can be easily recognised. It was taken to North Blyth when its working days were over and later transferred to Cambois. (J A Wells)

Chapter 11

Is Line Clear?

IN THE EARLIEST DAYS of railways there were no signals. At first this did not matter too much because trains moved slowly and were not very frequent but that situation did not last long. Drivers then had to be particularly vigilant and maintain a constant look out, though they soon evolved their own codes of handsignals for during the day. At night it was not unknown for them to throw a shovelful of red-hot cinders into the air to show their position! If a train was required to stop at an intermediate station flags might be used but at one location in County Durham they put a lighted candle in a window of the Station Master's house. If there was no candle the train could pass straight through. Sometimes drivers were assisted by hand signals given by railway policemen.

Various types of visual signals were tried of which the best known was the circular white board about two feet in diameter. If it was turned to face a train it meant 'stop' but end on it gave permission to proceed. The inadequacy of early signals and the danger of running on to facing points at junctions must have caused a great deal of stress to drivers, particularly as they were often fined if their train arrived late at its destination. In 1865, twenty-nine Gateshead drivers signed a letter to their Directors pointing out the hardship caused by those fines, complaining that train brakes were unreliable, platforms too short, signals could not easily be seen and that some station staff delayed trains unnecessarily.

Over a period of time semaphore signals were introduced. The Blyth & Tyne Railway Company made use of disc signals which were mounted above lamps with a white, green or red light for night use but even in 1858 they used a form of semaphore signal in which the arm stood out at right-angles to the post to denote 'danger'. If it pointed down at an angle of 45 degrees (or showed a *green* light) it indicated 'caution' and if the arm was concealed in a slot in the post it meant 'proceed'. Even then there was a compulsory interval of five minutes between trains, though this did not offer any protection should one break down after leaving a station.

On the North Eastern Railway Mr T E Harrison introduced in 1869 a mechanical device for wedging facing points and by 1872 all main line junctions and principal branches had been equipped. It was gradually extended to all routes thereby reducing the risk of the points moving under the weight of a passing train. Even then track layouts at many stations avoided facing points if at all possible in case a mechanical failure or other hazard caused a head-on collision. (Note:- 'Points' are where a line divides into two or more, as at junctions or sidings. If these face the direction of travel they are called *facing points;* if the train has to reverse over them they are known as *trailing points.*) The wedging of facing points was made even safer by interlocking them with signals so that routes had to be properly set before signals could be cleared for a train to move. Furthermore, if point blades were prevented from closing properly because of a stone or piece of coal the signal could not be changed until the failure was rectified.

Another major contribution to safety on the railways was the Absolute Block System in which each route was divided into *sections* controlled from a signal box. It had been introduced by the NER prior to 1871 on 48 miles of track between Darlington and Shildon and was

A wintery scene at Newsham circa 1910. The lines through the platforms lead to Morpeth and Newbiggin: the tracks on the right go to Blyth and the staiths. (Author's collection)

so successful that a decision was taken to extend it throughout their system. Considering the size of the Company and its determination to implement the other safety measures mentioned above, this was no mean task. Under the time-interval methods of running trains, the line was supposed to be clear after the previous train had been gone for five, ten or fifteen minutes. The Absolute Block System, however, assumed the line to be blocked until it was proved to be clear, and it allowed only one train in a section at a time. Before looking at this in more detail, it is worth making an imaginary visit to a typical signal-box to form a general impression of what railway signalling is all about, say in 1950 and earlier.

Entering the cabin one immediately sees a number of levers coming through slots in a curved, black, metal frame at floor level. The levers, standing some four feet high are painted in various colours. Each one has a polished, brass plate on the front bearing a number and indicating its use. On one may be 'Branch Down Home', on another 'Up Distant', a third might show 'Up Main to Down Main Crossover'. The colours classify their use in this way:-

RED levers operate *home* signals which protect all points, crossings and sidings, cover shunting movements, and allow trains to pass from one section to another.

YELLOW are for *distant* signals which are placed up to one mile in the rear of the 'box to give drivers preliminary notice as to whether the next home signal is clear or at danger.

BLACK ones are for changing points.

BLUE levers are used alongside black ones when facing points are involved. These are locking bars to wedge the points. To use, the lever is normally pulled forward to release the interlocking, the black lever to change the points is also pulled forward then the lock lever is pushed back.

BROWN is for releasing or locking wheels for turning level-crossing gates, also for wicket gates.

WHITE levers are spare and not in use.

Above the frame hangs a large track diagram showing the layout of the lines, the position of every point and signal, and the situation of any level crossing gates. Each one is numbered to correspond with those on the levers. On one side of each lever is painted the numbers of others which have to be pulled before that particular one. In some signal boxes the position of trains is indicated on the track diagram by red panels which light up as the train progresses. These are known as track circuits.

On a stout, polished shelf above the lever frame are various pieces of equipment, the most obvious of which are block bells and block instruments. Briefly, these are used to pass messages from one signal box to another and to show whether trains are in the section. When a particular signal cannot be seen from the cabin, a small dial on the front of the shelf will repeat the state of the signal, showing whether it is ON (for danger), OFF (for clear) or WRONG. The latter means the signal is not giving a proper indication to drivers in that the arm is somewhere between being 'on' and 'off'.

Every signal box has at least two telephones. Some of these are quite ancient, having a listening piece separate from the speaker. Contact with other signalmen is made by lifting the receiver and pressing the contact button, using the appropriate code, similar to morse. The code for one particular 'box might be long-short-long, another may be five short; a third, long-three short. The signalman hearing the call sign for his cabin on the buzzer would answer. Others could listen in if they were so inclined, so to prevent this men in adjacent 'boxes sometimes used an unofficial code on the block bell (1 pause 1) meaning "Come to the phone". Railway telephones of this type dated from North Eastern days but were used by the LNER and for some years by British Railways before being replaced by more modern equipment. A larger type of telephone connects the signal box with the Control in Newcastle.

Each signal box is given a 3-aspect handlamp for use at night. This can show white, green or red and is a means of giving information to a driver to supplement signals. For emergency use there are red and green flags, also detonators. Some cabins can place detonators on the line by pulling up a handle on the frame but this is only used to warn drivers of unforeseen danger.

The desk in a 'cabin, with a clock above it mounted on the wall, is probably standard issue with a sloping top on which rests the Train Register Book. Every bell signal passed and received is entered in there as a record, the only exception being 'call attention'. Inside the desk is the Occurrence Book, a file of permanent notices and information about track repairs, special trains, alterations to arrange- ments, vacancy lists - that sort of thing.

The basic requirements for the Absolute Block System are a block bell and a block instrument for each 'section' on the line. If a particular signal box works to two others there are two each of these: if there is a junction and it works to three others then there are three of each.

At its simplest let us consider three signal boxes 'A', 'B', and 'C' along a route. A train, let us say a stopping passenger train, is preparing to leave 'A'. The signalman there goes to the block bell connected to 'B' and gives one beat. This is the Call Attention signal which rings on the bell in 'B'. The signalman there answers with one beat, which rings in 'A'. From 'A', 3 pause 1 is tapped out and again this rings out in 'B'. It is saying, "Is your line clear for a stopping passenger train?" If the line is not clear the signal is ignored. If it is clear the signal is repeated, 3 - 1.

The block instrument - with variations in different parts of the country - has two identical dials and a small knob protruding on the face of a third dial, in a vertical line. Each dial is divided into 3 sections marked "LINE BLOCKED", "LINE CLEAR" and "TRAIN ON LINE". On receiving the bell signal and repeating it, the signalman at 'B' has accepted the train. He then turns the knob to LINE CLEAR. The needle on the lower dial on his block instrument now points also to LINE CLEAR, so does that on the upper dial in Box 'A'. Without this the appropriate signals at 'A' are locked electrically at danger. When the line clear is given the locks are released and the signalman can pull off his signals, giving the driver permission to proceed.

As the train is leaving, 'A' gives 2 beats on the bell to 'B' - this is the Train Entering Section signal. 'B' repeats this and turns the indicator to TRAIN ON LINE. Again the needle on the lower dial in Box 'B' and that on the upper dial in 'A' point to TRAIN ON LINE. When it is in that position the section is occupied and another train cannot be offered nor could the signalman pull off the signal controlling entry into the next section because of the electric locking. The signals at 'A' are returned to danger as the train passes them, meanwhile the signalman at 'B' calls the attention of 'C', on the block bell connected to that cabin. This is answered on the block bell, 1 beat. 3 - 1 is then given - "Is your line clear for a stopping passenger train?" If yes, the signal is repeated, and the LINE CLEAR is displayed in both signal boxes as previously explained. At this stage the lower dial of one block instrument in box 'B' shows TRAIN ON LINE from 'A' and the upper dial of the other instrument denotes LINE CLEAR from 'C'. He is able to clear his signals by pulling over the appropriate levers.

As the train approaches and passes 'B' the Train Entering Section

The Signal Gantry, looking south from Newsham station, shows home, distant and shunting signals. The two distant signals are worked from Newsham South and when in the 'off' position show drivers they have a clear run through the next section. 1967. (J A Wells)

is given to 'C' (2 beats) which is acknowledged and the block instrument there is turned to TRAIN ON LINE. The signalman at 'B' observes that all is well with the train (no carriage doors open, etc.) and above all that the last vehicle carries a tail lamp. He then returns to the block bell to 'A', calls attention, and when answered gives the Train out of Section signal, 2 pause 1, and returns his indicator to LINE BLOCKED. Again his lower dial shows the same, as does the upper dial in Box 'A'. 'A' could then offer another train which may have been held at signals.

At 'C' the signalman offers the train to 'D', clears his signals and follows the procedures described above. Similarly if he is satisfied all is well with the train, including the tail-lamp (which shows the train is complete) he calls attention to 'B', gives the Train out of Section signal and returns the block instrument to LINE BLOCKED.

Below is a selection of bell codes used by the LNER, and, later, the
Eastern Region of British Railways:-

	BELL
IS LINE CLEAR FOR	CODE
Express passenger train; Officers' Special (passing through); breakdown train or snowplough train going to clear the line; engine going to assist a disabled train	4 consec.
Stopping passenger train; breakdown train (etc) not going to clear line	3-1
Empty coaching stock	2-2-1
Express parcels, milk, fish, fruit, livestock, etc. fully braked	1-3-1
Light engine or light engines coupled and with no more than two brake vans attached	2-3
(NB shortly after nationalisation an engine with not more than two brake vans attached was signalled 1-1-3. Light engines continued to be 2-3)	
Mineral or empty wagon train	4-1

Various other bell codes were used to cover all eventualities
including emergencies, some of which are:-

Obstruction - danger!	6 consec.
Stop and examine train	7 consec.
Train passed without tail lamp	9 consec to 'box in advance: 4-5 to 'box in rear.
Shunt train for following train to pass	1-5-5
Train or vehicles running away in wrong direction	2-5-5
Time signal	8-5-5
Testing of bells and instruments	16 consec.

With five exceptions, the 'call attention' signal had to be given in
each case. The exemptions were:-
Train entering section: Obstruction - danger!:
Assisting engine in rear of train: Stop & Examine Train: Time
Signal.
A trainee signalman about to take an examination would remember
the initial letters of these spelt T O A S T.

The classification of a train in steam days was shown by the
arrangement of lamps on the locomotive, or tender if it was running

tender first. There were four lamp brackets - one above each buffer, one in the centre of the buffer beam and one below the chimney, or equivalent position on the tender - and the placing of one or two headlamps denoted the type of train. Royal trains carried a lamp on all four brackets.

A signalman needs a thorough knowledge not only of the various bell codes and numerous regulations but also of the gradients and the different emergency procedures appertaining to the particular location. His duties are to receive or pass trains from one section to another in complete safety and enable any shunting movements to be carried out. It is necessary to watch passing trains for such things as signs of distress by passengers, carriage doors open, axle-boxes running hot, objects which might fall from a goods train, or a load which has moved so as to obstruct another line; indeed anything likely to affect safety. A signalman would also ensure that his signals were properly lit. These all had a container for a supply of oil which would normally last a week with continuous burning. Usually this was a kind of rape oil, also called long-burning oil or simply signal oil. The wicks were trimmed when the new oil was put in. In some places this work was done by a lamp-man covering a small area who would take replenished lamps to each signal or ground signal and take out from the lamp housing the one which needed replacing and servicing. These would then be taken back to the lamp room, often situated under the structure of a water storage tank. If there was no lamp-man it was one of the duties of a porter to do this. At night home and shunting signals showed a red light. The small ground signals incidentally, used between tracks where there was not room for a conventional signal, were known as *dollies*. Distant signals showed an orange light at night. When in the 'off' position all signals showed green by the simple expedient of the moving arm holding a blue glass in front of the yellow flame of the lamp. How could the signalman be sure a signal lamp was lit when it faced away from him? The signal engineers of the past had thought of that, too. They made a very small window at the back of the lamp housing which showed a white light just big enough to be seen from the signal box. This was always called a *back-board* - and by cleverly including a small shield to cover the light when the arm moved to 'off', it enabled a signalman to know the signal was functioning correctly. If, then, the signal was at 'danger' and he could see the back-light, the lamp was lit and showing red. If he could not see it, the lamp had gone out. If the signal was 'off' there would be no light visible to him.

Some entries from Occurrence Books have already been considered, particularly in connection with specific locomotives but as these can give an additional insight into railway working a further selection will not come amiss:-

WOODHORN COLLIERY JCN.

Sept. 1st 1896	Received half a truck of unscreened coals.No. of wagon 1691.
May 16th 1897	9.15 pm passenger train ex Newbiggin stopped 4 or 5 minutes at Woodhorn Bridge. Ashington wired saying a man had been killed.
Jan. 17th 1902	Received old carriage mat today.
Aug. 29th 1903	Received Stop & Examine signal from Hirst Jcn. at 8.54 for the 7.36 pm relief train ex New Bridge St. When stopped I found a carriage door open. Train delayed 2 mins.
Sept. 12th 1903	The 6.58 pm Passenger Train stopped here 7 minutes. Through The Brakes getting Fast. (As written.)

HIRST JCN.

Oct. 28th 1905	Policeman Briggs informed me at 11.17 pm that driver of the 11.13 pm Passenger had struck something on line between Bedlington & No. Seaton. I telegraphed to Bedlington and was answered back that he had struck some sleepers laid across the line and that the keys were out of the rails.
Jan. 30th 1913	Very foggy from 7.30 am. Fogmen Speedy and Foggan on duty 8.20 - 9.30 am.
Oct. 31st 1914	As goods was leaving for Newbiggin at 9.43 am Porter R Gibson went through the bridge with a one-wheeled barrow. He was turning the corner when goods passed him. Engine cleared him, but the handle of a wagon brake caught the barrow and turned him over and over to the middle of the bridge. Barrow smashed and Gibson bruised on head and legs. Goods stopped to see if he was alright and left at 9.48 am.

NEWSHAM NORTH

Nov. 5th 1911   Received 'Obstruction Danger' signal ex Plessey Road Box at 1.43 pm. A large wooden case having been blown on the line. It being a very stormy day. 'Obstruction Removed' received 1.52 pm.

Dec. 10th 1911   Horse killed at Isabella Jct. by 9.58 pm Down passenger. Little delay to train.

(June, July, Aug.   1912 Several entries regarding re-signalling and considerable re-laying of track at Newsham.)

Aug. 23rd 1916   An English airship passed over Newsham Station in the direction of Blyth from Percy Main. (N.B. A German Zeppelin was reported over Blyth and Choppington on April 14th 1915: it later raided Howdon and Jarrow.)

Nov. 11th 1918   End of War news at 10 am. Peace flags flying, buzzers blowing, rockets fired from ships in Blyth Harbour.

June 28th 1919   As the 7.36 pm Car was leaving the station I observed a carriage door being opened by a girl. I immediately placed the Up Advanced Starting signal to danger and stopped the Car. Before the Car was brought to a stand the girl jumped out and fell in the six-foot way. I promptly ran to her assistance and on reaching her found her rather shaken but not seriously hurt. The Car was delayed about three minutes in consequence.

Oct. 20th 1925   Informed by fireman of engine 1842 at 8.42 that wagon on fire in No. 1 siding. Taken to water column by engine 1933.

Jan. 13th 1930   Received nine pen nibs today for cabin use. S. Anderson: signal lad.

Aug. 22nd 1933   Driver of 11.40 am Newbiggin to Manors reported sheep on line between here and Bebside at 12.7 pm.

July 31st 1936   Pigeon Special delayed 9.13 - 9.20. No. 29 points out of order.

Feb. 2nd 1941   Engine 767 working 5.25 am goods ex Heaton to Ashington ran through Plessey Road gates at

8.20 am owing to No. 67 signal sticking to 'off'
position. Distant disconnected 9 am.

Nov. 30th 1942   Guard and fireman supplied with rations 11.5
pm. Train Control advised. Engine 428, cattle.

Jan. 17th 1945   Coal train ex Crofton arrived 8.13 pm. Informed
by Guard that train had divided. 'Vehicles running
away on wrong line' sent to Isabella Box, 8.13 pm.
Rear portion collided with an engine and van 2354
following up from New Blyth.

Mar. 15th 1947   Up and Down lines under Engineer's Orders, 2
pm. Snow ploughs working to Bedlington.

Dec. 28th 1955   Derailment at Bebside Station. Both lines
blocked. Obstruction Danger received from
Bebside 2.54 pm. Obstruction removed 8.59 pm.
(When a signalman sends the 'Obstruction-Danger'
signal he immediately turns the block instrument
to Train on Line, ensuring no other train can be sent
through until the Obstruction Removed signal, 2-1,
is given.)

From time to time Occurrence Books recorded the number of *moves*
made with levers in the course of a day or two days. This may have
been done to re-assess the classification of a signal-box for wages
purposes, or it may have been an appraisal of how well equipment
was working. The following is an entry from the Woodhorn Colliery
Junction book:-

Oct. 25th 1912   Moves taken today.

6 am	—	7 am	27
7 am	—	8 am	85
8 am	—	9 am	120
9 am	—	10 am	80
10 am	—	11 am	82
11 am	—	12 noon	76
12 noon	—	1 pm	104
1 pm	—	2 pm	73
2 pm	—	3 pm	94
3 pm	—	4 pm	173
4 pm	—	5 pm	55
5 pm	—	6 pm	63
6 pm	—	7 pm	30
7 pm	—	8 pm	69

8 pm	—	9 pm	44
9 pm	—	10 pm	55
10 pm	—	11 pm	49
11 pm	—	12 mid.	69

TOTAL MOVES   1348
NUMBER OF TRAINS   59
AVERAGE MOVES PER TRAIN   22

Hirst Junction recorded 2,179 moves on October 29 1912.
An analysis of 'marks' taken at Newsham North on June 18/19 1924
included:-

5,234   lever movements
971   train signalling
140   hand signals, etc.

The number of trains on the two days was shown as 250.
Many signal-boxes on the North Eastern Railway were equipped
with a single-needle Telegraph Instrument as a means of passing

*Bedlington North was one of the larger signal boxes on the Blyth &
Tyne Branch. It is situated at the junction of the Morpeth and
Ashington branches. At one time it had 64 levers and three sets of level
crossing gates. (J A Wells)*

messages, a system used on the main line north from Newcastle as
early as 1846 or 1847. A wooden handle to fit neatly into a closed hand
had a limited movement to the left and right. When this was done the
needle above also moved to left or right and was repeated in other
signal-boxes along the route and in the Telegraph Office. Each letter
of the alphabet was coded to enable messages to be sent. These
continued in use for at least a hundred years. For the sake of brevity,
code words were devised to replace groups of words, sentences, or
even a whole paragraph in certain situations. Each signal-box was
provided with a booklet giving the numerous codes under different
headings. Significantly these, or similar ones, were still used for
telegrams on railway business in the 1960s. A random selection is
included as being of historical interest:-

MINT   Undermentioned cannot take duty. Arrange.
CABBAGE   Do you agree to the following?
LOOT   Undermentioned wagons of live ——— left here on
           train named. Work forward all speed.
SHAMBLE   Arrange to feed and water at ———.
LYRIC   Theatrical special between following points next
           Sunday.
ANCHOVY   Collect fare from passenger without ticket in
           undermentioned train hence.
CASTER   Down main line blocked.
HB   Horse box.
FURNO   Until further notice.
CORBEX   Can you provide a train of open seconds for
           following excursion?
SNIPE   Send supply of loco coal to ——— first means.
DERAIL   Send quickly breakdown van, crane and gang;
           following derailed at (insert place and time).
CLOTH   Be prepared to detach undermentioned leaving
           here next to locomotive on following train.
ACK   Acknowledge receipt by wire.
GUITAR   Wire particulars and confirm by letter.

These would be used in this way:-
        (1) CLOTH HB 5-20 pm EX MANORS TODAY ACK.
        (2) DERAIL 952 FURNACE WAY 11.10 am CASTER.

An experienced operator could send and receive messages very
quickly but others not so proficient needed to watch and listen very
carefully and acknowledge each word. The telegraph instrument was

sometimes referred to by signalmen on the Branch as 'the speaker'.

* * * * * * *

The signal-boxes on the Blyth & Tyne Branch varied in size and shape but basically were built of brick with plenty of sliding windows in wooden frames above. In the under-cabin were the rods, levers, cranks, pulleys and wires for working the signals and points, together with (in earlier days) numerous single-cell batteries in square jars which were used until more modern methods were introduced. A comparison between two signal boxes on contrasting parts of the branch, again about 1950, will serve to emphasise that, although conforming to the same basic pattern all are different in detail.

BENTON. Benton 'box, which had 39 levers, worked to four others, consequently there were four block instruments and four block bells each with a distinctive sound. Because of the short distance to Benton East all Up trains from Backworth were immediately offered on to South Gosforth East as soon as they had been accepted from Benton East. If the normal procedure was followed and bell signals were passed on only when Train Entering Section was received from the latter, there would have been no time to pull signals off and each train would be pulling up before the signals were cleared. With the exception of some shunting during the night, most trains passed through Benton. With a twenty minute service of electric trains in each direction, expresses at peak times, empty stock movements, some coal trains, and passenger trains to and from Newbiggin, plus occasional trains from the north this was always a busy cabin. Extra complications could arise when main line trains were diverted via the north west curve. Another interesting variation was when the turntable at Heaton sheds was out of order. When that happened, strings of engines, up to eight or nine at a time, would travel up the south west curve into the station. Mighty 'Pacifics' with lanky wheels rubbed buffers with little shunters or dirty coal engines. They crossed to the Down line then proceeded to Benton East, and from there round the south east curve back up the main line to Heaton, all being turned in the process. The bell signal used for these straggles of locomotives was 2 - 3 for the first one, followed by the Train Entering Section signal as they passed from on section to another, then 2 - 2 (engine assisting in rear of train) to be given and acknowledged for each engine after that. For a group of six, therefore, the sequence of signals given from one cabin to the next would be:-

          1 (1 in reply): 2 - 3 (acknowledged if accepted):
          2 (train on line; ack.):
          2 - 2 (repeated); 2 - 2 (repeated); 2 - 2 (repeated);
          2 - 2 (repeated); 2 - 2 (repeated): later 2 - 1 for train out
          of section.

BEDLINGTON NORTH. Because of the single platform for passenger trains and the need for many coal trains to reverse direction at the junction, Bedlington North had to work closely with its neighbour, Bedlington South. As it had 65 levers and three sets of level crossing gates there were two men on both shifts during the day, but only one at night. Each man worked back shift, front shift, back, front, nights, in that rotation, consequently each one worked with two others out of the remaining four. With one he was charge-man who made the decisions; with the other he was what *they* called 'the laddie'!

An extra block bell between the North and South cabins meant that 'direction' codes could be given without recourse to the telephone. The driver of a set of empties, for example, passing Bebside would whistle 1 for the Morpeth direction, 2 for the branch towards Newbiggin. When the South box offered the train to the North cabin they would also give 1 or 2 beats on the extra bell and the signalmen in the latter would 'set the road' accordingly. Similarly, a train passing Choppington would whistle once for straight through Bedlington, four 'pops' for the Furnace Way sidings, or 1 - 2 - 2 if it needed to run round its train before proceeding down the branch. This was relayed by telephone and the signal was passed on to Bedlington South so that the men there knew where the train was going.

Bedlington was one of the signal boxes that reported the movement of mineral and goods trains to Control. The messages given were just enough to give basic details:-

"Control? Aye, Bedlington North here. 65815 passed here 3.11 pm with empties for Morpeth." Or

". . . 65797 arrived here 10.17 am from Choppington, departed 10.30 for North Blyth."

In the Control the movement of every engine and every train was recorded on a 24-hour graph divided into two-minute intervals, specially fitted to unroll over a sheet of glass. Booked trains were already printed on but a running record of the position of other trains was built up as their passing times were reported from signal-boxes. The progress of each was plotted by coloured lines, according to the class of train, with horizontal red lines being used for signal checks. The Blyth & Tyne Branch was one of nine areas covered by different controllers. Signal boxes were shown down the side of the graph and trains in both directions were plotted. Control, having the full, current picture of all traffic could advise signalmen which train should have priority or be held back; they could make the best use of engines, and in emergencies could arrange diversions, cancellations or whatever alterations were necessary. This system was pioneered in the North Eastern Area of the LNER.

Bedlington North was one of the cabins that received the time check on the telegraph instrument over many years, dead on 10 o'clock every morning, and passed this on immediately to Bedlington South, Choppington and West Sleekburn cabins by ringing 8 - 5 - 5 on the block bells, one man doing two bells together, one with each hand. When all three replied simultaneously it made quite a racket sometimes to the consternation of people outside!

Level crossing gates at this 'box were in constant use. Of the three sets, two had four gates each and were quite easy to handle but the pair for the bay platform and sidings were heavy to turn particularly in a strong wind. When traffic was at a peak the 'branch' and 'main line' gates were opened and shut frequently in an effort to keep both rail and road vehicles on the move.

A signalman's job was certainly a responsible one but he needed the co-operation of signal-fitters, linemen, interlocking experts, platelayers and others - every one of them was essential for the railway to be efficient.

Although manual signal-boxes are still in use on branches such as the Blyth & Tyne, main lines now have colour-light signalling, modern safety devices and a few highly-technical signal boxes covering several miles. Automatic colour light signals and equipment which can detect any vehicle on the track mean that the old block system is no longer required on such lines and a section of track is now assumed to be CLEAR unless it is shown to be occupied and, therefore, electrically protected. It is no longer necessary to have telephone poles with numerous wires between every signal box.

In February 1964 points and signals worked by Manors North, Jesmond and West Jesmond were transferred to Newcastle signal box. The following month Benton, Benton East and Backworth were put on the new panel at Benton box, situated at Benton Quarry on the main line, and some colour light signals were installed instead of semaphores. On the Branch, level crossings were gradually phased out and replaced by barriers, some operated from a distance with the aid of television cameras. Plessey Road Crossing at Newsham first came under Newsham North but when that 'box was phased out in August 1977 the barriers were operated from Newsham South. The last remaining level crossing, at Bebside, was replaced in the mid 1980s.

Block instrument & Block Bell. These are an integral part of the Absolute Block System, a very safe and reliable method of train control. (J A Wells)

Chapter 12

"Off The Road"

OFF THE ROAD is the railwayman's term for a derailment. A simple derailment can involve a locomotive partly or totally off the track, but upright; a coach which may have tried to go two ways at points during shunting; or from one to a few wagons whose wheels, or some of them, have dropped off the track for one reason or another. Such derailments can be caused by wrongly set points (particularly where these are not operated from the signal cabin) or by too vigorous shunting, a 'snatch' of couplings, poor communications, misunderstandings, or sheer carelessness. Nevertheless, it is a comparatively simple task to rerail vehicles using ramps, jacks or a crane. More serious accidents have been caused by such things as excessive speed, drivers mis-reading or failing to observe signals, trains not pulling up in time, runaway vehicles, or a signalman forgetting about a train he has standing and allowing another one to run into it because rules were ignored.

Apart from the considerable cost of replacing track and vehicles, such derailments can cause serious disruption to traffic which has a knock-on effect over a very large area. If one line of a double track route is blocked it may be possible for single line working to be introduced. In the past this would normally be put into operation by the Station Master and either he or another competent person would act as *Pilotman*. The latter had to wear a broad, red armlet, bearing the word PILOTMAN in white letters, above the elbow of his left arm. No train was allowed through the section where single line working was in operation unless accompanied by the Pilotman, or unless he personally had given the driver specific permission to proceed. This was done when more than one train was required to pass through in the same direction.

Every section of railway has had its share of derailments over the years and the Blyth & Tyne Branch is no exception. Taken together, these may look formidable but it must be remembered they do span quite a number of years.

A signalman who was offered a train on the block bell would accept

it, if his line was clear, by repeating the signal. If he could not accept
it because his line was not clear the bell signal would be temporarily
ignored. A regulation did allow for freight, mineral trains and light
engines to be taken *at caution,* in this way:-

Again, 'A', 'B', and 'C' are three signal boxes. 'C' has offered 'B' a
train of mineral empties (bell code 4 - 1) and this he has accepted.
As the train passes 'C' he rings 2 beats on the bell to 'B' - the Train
Entering Section (or Train on Line) signal. 'B' then goes to the block
bell connected to 'A' and gives 1 beat (call attention). 'A' replies and
is offered 4 - 1. It may be that the signalman there has a train shunting
which is occupying part of the running line, or that he has one coming
out of sidings. His line is not clear so he could decide not to answer
the bell code immediately, in which case the train would be halted
at 'B'. If the chance is that the section will be clear very soon 'A' can
reply 3 - 5 - 5 on the bell which is saying, "I'll take this train but tell
him I may have to stop him here." This bell signal must be repeated
before the Train on Line signal is given. On receiving 3 - 5 - 5 the
signalman at 'B' has to do two things. First he must slow the train
down by the signals until it has nearly stopped, and as it approaches
him hold a green flag steadily out of the cabin window, or a green
light if at night. This is acknowledged by the driver with a pop on the
engine whistle. He now understands he may be stopped in the next
section and will regulate his speed accordingly. The use of a green
signal goes back to the days when green meant 'caution' and white
'all clear'. In December 1923 just before 4 am such a signal had been
given at Benton to the driver of an Up coal train hauled by an unfitted
P 3 class 0-6-0, later J27. The train proceeded at reduced speed and
was brought to a stand at South Gosforth East's home signal.
Meanwhile an empty electric train had drawn out of the car sheds and
stood on the Down line waiting for permission to move through the
crossover and travel on to Newcastle ahead of the coal train. Once
the coal train had been stopped the points were changed to allow the
electric set through and the signal was changed accordingly. The
advance signal was also cleared but the driver of the coal train
mistook this as being for him and also moved forward. The engine
collided with the third coach as it negotiated the crossover and,
somewhat surprisingly, left the rails, ploughed along the embankment for a few yards, overturned and fell into the road below the
bridge it was on. The tender came to rest across the cab and both
crewmen were killed. The loco was recovered the following day by

breakdown cranes from Gateshead and Darlington. The new car sheds at South Gosforth were brought into use on 30 September 1923 and the crossover had been put in less than a fortnight earlier. The unfortunate driver, who was within a year of his retirement, had gone past a signal still at danger, with tragic consequences.

Another incident where a driver missed seeing an intermediate signal happened at Bedlington North one dark evening in the mid 1940's, during a particularly busy spell. An engine ran into the rear of a stationary coal train causing the brake van and three loaded wagons to jump off the track and become buffer-locked.

On a running line with a rising gradient one way of intercepting any runaway vehicles is by putting in catch points, sometimes called trap points. These are spring loaded so that any vehicles travelling in the right direction pass through safely but if there is a breakaway and trucks run backwards they are turned off the track before they can do too much damage. A similar device is used where lines converge on to a running line. In this case a train which did not stop in time would be in danger of hitting another one passing by, so to prevent this it is diverted on to run-off points (or *jacks*) and derailed. Such safety points existed at the entrance to the two collieries at Bedlington Station, near Bedlington South, though in this case there were stout buffer stops to give some protection to the footbridge beside the level crossing. In the early 1940s an LNER long-wheelbase brake van ran out of the colliery sidings and after hitting the buffer stops with considerable force came to rest almost on end beside the bridge. In January 1949 a similar thing happened when four empty wagons tore up the same buffer stops after running away from the Doctor Pit. The leading coal truck shot up to a near-vertical position on impact, the next two were shattered but the fourth one was hardly damaged. One side of the bridge was torn away though no-one was hurt.

In March 1949 part of a goods train quickly gathered momentum when it ran away from Earsdon Junction, crashed through the gates at Holywell and careered down the hill to Seghill crossing where the wagons crashed head on with an oncoming NCB train at a speed estimated at 60 mph. Press reports indicated twelve wagons were involved, including two 1,500 gallon tankers loaded with paraffin and at least one open truck filled with bones from a slaughter house. The colliery train they hit was a load of seventeen wagons of coal from Seaton Delaval to the Tyne, hauled by the former Hartley Main Collieries loco number 6. The tender, which took the force of the

Moving forward against a signal at danger resulted in this P3 crashing into the road below, with tragic consequences, in 1923. The ornate bridge sides date from 1864 and one side is still intact at South Gosforth today. (Northumberland County Record Office)

When an 0-6-0 tank engine belonging to the NCB overran a signal at Fisher Lane, near Backworth, in 1963 it overturned BR J27 Number 65812. (G E Charlton)

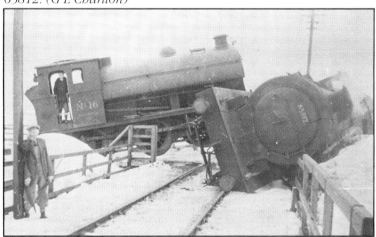

impact, was badly damaged and was surrounded by the wreckage of the splintered trucks. In the darkness, the driver and fireman had no chance to jump clear though this in itself undoubtedly saved their lives and they escaped with minor injuries. One suggestion at the time as to the cause of this accident was that when the engine was shunting wagons at Earsdon the guard may have released the brakes on his van prematurely. When the engine backed on to its train with other wagons he would intend to couple up and wait for the train to move forward, when he would jump on to the step of the brake van as it passed him. On this occasion it was thought the couplings did not engage first time but the nudge of buffers was sufficient to send the stationary wagons rolling backwards.

On another occasion, the signalman at Seghill North, having received the 'Train or vehicles running away on wrong line' signal, was able to open his gates, change the points and divert the runaways into a siding where they demolished the buffer-stops and ended up in the cricket field.

A collision on the staiths at North Blyth in January 1950 caused three coal wagons to plunge over the side and three others, including a 42-ton hopper, to be derailed, thereby delaying the loading of ships at four berths. A newspaper report claimed a string of wagons hit some empty trucks and sent them crashing into another line of empties. The big truck hung precariously over the side and was only prevented from crashing on to the jetty below by the coupling holding it to another wagon. It was re-railed after being lifted from its dangerous position with hydraulic jacks by the Percy Main crew. Their crane could not be used at that location and recovery of the three wagons would, said the report, "present a delicate task".

At Newcastle Central, platforms 1, 2 and 3 handled the majority of services on the North Tyneside electrified area. Trains travelling out via Benton returned via Wallsend and vice-versa. With a train leaving every twenty minutes on both routes, plus a corresponding number returning, there was traffic in or out every five minutes, more at peak periods. The four tracks between Newcastle and Manors always carried heavy traffic including main line passenger and freight trains. From time to time slight delays occurred, as for example when an incoming train needed a platform, or when a train due to depart was held back owing to congestion on the bridge to Manors. In August 1951 a train from the coast via Wallsend was entering platform 1 under clear signals when it was struck by the 10.35 am departure

which had moved out of platform 2 against a signal at red. The cab
of the incoming train was wrecked in this slow-speed collision and
the driver was trapped for three hours. He and one passenger died
and 43 passengers were injured, 21 of whom required hospital
treatment. Most of the injuries were caused because people were
standing up or moving to the exit doors prior to alighting.

Two other derailments at Manors can be mentioned in passing even
though one is not really relative to the Blyth & Tyne Branch. In August
1973 a train conveying heavy fuel oil from a refinery on Teesside to
Scotland, travelling at normal speed through the station failed to
negotiate a crossover between platforms at Manors East. Six of the
eight 100-ton tankers were derailed when the rear bogie of the first
one left the track and pulled others after it. Rumours at the time
suggested the screw coupling between it and the diesel locomotive
was too tight, thereby restricting movement, but this has not been
verified.

In February 1974 another spectacular mishap occurred at Manors,
this time on the bridge, when a train of empty coal wagons from the
Blaydon area, west of Newcastle, heading to Blyth via Heaton and the
south east curve at Benton, became derailed near the ancient Keep.
A pair of wheels on a wagon about eighth from the end of the train
left the rails and it bounced along for some two hundred yards before
hitting part of the parapet. The train divided and three wagons
plunged over the wall, coming to rest one on top of the other at the
foot of a multi-storey car park and damaging cables. Others behind
them also went 'off the road' - but the rest of the train carried on until
it was stopped at Heaton about a mile further on. It is possible that
this derailment was caused as a result of rapid acceleration which
made some slack couplings towards the rear of the train tighten too
quickly, causing a severe jerk. Had this train been fitted with brakes
worked from the engine both parts would have stopped automatically once the brake hoses were severed.

The most serious accident on the Branch happened in 1959 at West
Sleekburn, situated about a mile beyond Bedlington station on the
way to Newbiggin. In that year 40 to 45 coal trains a day would pass
the signal box, plus sixteen passenger or parcels trains. Normally, if
one train had to cross in front of another it was only allowed to do
so when the second one had been stopped. West Sleekburn was one
of the junctions for coal trains travelling to Cambois and North Blyth:
it also handled trains from the collieries on either side. Because it was

situated in a dip, it was necessary, as far as possible, for loaded trains on the Down line from Bedlington to be given a clear run through the junction to enable them take the gradient on the right without assistance from another locomotive. For safety reasons, a special regulation required any train on the Up line from North Seaton, which had been accepted 'at caution' by West Sleekburn, to be actually *stopped* at Marcheys House before being shown the green flag or light and allowed to proceed.

At 7.22 pm on 4 November 1959 a Down mineral train for North Blyth approached the junction under clear signals at 25-30 mph. It consisted of a J27 locomotive, number 65824, which weighed about 78 tons, and 24 wagons plus two brake vans, a load of 733 tons. It was 220 yards long. An Up coal train with two 13-ton wagons, twenty 16-tonners and a brake van, 532 tons in total and 169 yards in length, had been stopped at Marcheys House and sent forward at caution. Although travelling slowly the engine, 65847, another J27, failed to stop and skidded past the signal at danger even though the fireman had tried to pin down some wagon brakes and the driver did try to put his engine into reverse. He did not have time to whistle for braking assistance from the guard who did not realise anything was wrong. As both engines had had the leading left buffer wrenched off it was assumed that they were the first point of contact. The Up train was moving at walking pace but the touch was sufficient to cause a major pile up. Its engine was tipped over but no wagons left the track and there was little damage. The other train, however, was much less fortunate. The locomotive came to rest on its side thirty yards along the branch: the tender, pushed by the momentum of the wagons, was badly distorted and lay projecting into the upper part of the cab, its body almost separated from the chassis. The leading brake van and the first three wagons were wrecked and the next three suffered severe damage. The rest of the train remained on the track though the impact caused the bottom doors of some wagons to burst open. Owing to the original signal box being burnt down some weeks earlier, temporary arrangements involved the use of an inspector and flagmen, but this had not contributed to the accident which caused the death of a driver and his fireman. In order to get the traffic moving again the damaged loco and wagons were placed at the side of the track and removed at later date.

During the Second World War a coal train from Bedlington had passed over the same junction heading for North Blyth but the engine slipped to a halt on the gradient. The driver eased back a little to make another attempt but in doing so caused a brake van and three wagons to be derailed at the safety points.

Another derailment occurred at West Sleekburn in August 1973 when a class 37 diesel, number 6768, over-ran a signal at danger. Having taken a load of coal to Blyth power station it was returning towards Bedlington with a train of empties. When the driver did not stop at the home signal protecting the junction, the locomotive, leading brake van and one wagon left the track at the run-off points, the diesel leaning over at 45 degrees. The brake van and the 21-ton hopper were rerailed without difficulty and taken away but the loco needed the combined efforts of the 75-ton Gateshead crane and the 45-ton one from Thornaby, Teesside, the following Sunday. Both crews were on site by 7 am.

The Thornaby crane first lifted its own jib-runner on to the adjacent track out of the way then disposed of one of the relieving bogies in the same manner, enabling work to proceed unhindered. With outriggers in position and jibs well aloft the next task was to firmly attach the slings to the diesel. Lifting was then done slowly and deliberately in unison to give the loco a chance to level out and hang upright. It was necessary for the rear end of the 37 to be held just above the track by the Gateshead crane so that a minor misalignment in the rails could be corrected.

Rerailing was completed at 10.45 am and 6768 was placed between the two breakdown trains which then travelled to Bedlington for re-marshalling. The complete train leaving the site was thus made up as follows:-

> 2 breakdown train units from Thornaby depot
> Thornaby loco
> Thornaby tool van
> Thornaby 45-ton steam crane
> Loco 6768
> Gateshead 75-ton crane
> 3 Gateshead breakdown train units
> Gateshead loco.

At Holywell signal box a double junction took tracks to Burradon. Along this line there was an unusual intersection where two lines crossed in a level crossing at Fisher Lane. It was there in 1963 that another J27, number 65812 was bumped by an NCB tank engine and knocked off the track. The small, colliery signal box there was also

*Steam cranes from Gateshead and Thornaby rerailing a class 37
diesel at West Sleekburn, 1973. (J A Wells)*

the scene of a murder some years later.

Couplings between wagons are immensely strong but with loose-coupled trains there is a danger that too sudden a jerk could cause a wagon to give a little jump. If the wheels landed back on the rails all was well, if not it spelt trouble. A good driver would always get his train on the move gradually and with a steam engine could sense when the couplings were taut before increasing speed. It was a case of an ounce of practice being worth a ton of theory! With a diesel locomotive it was not so easy. An *instanter* coupling, while still being three link, could be used in the long or short position, the latter keeping the wagons closer together. What may have been a jolt caused several wagons to be toppled on to their sides at Newsham in 1978 and track to be torn up. A length of rail was forced right through one of the steel 24½ ton hopper wagons from one end to the other, and into the end of the next wagon, this in spite of it being loaded with fine coal.

At Morpeth there have been three major disasters on the main line at the notorious curve. In March 1877 five people died and ten were badly injured when a broken fish plate (used for joining lengths of rail) caused a night express to leave the track at the south end of the station. The engine, built five years before, was a Fletcher 2-4-0, number 901, and was hauling an open fish wagon, two luggage vans, a sleeping carriage, seven East Coast Joint Stock coaches and a guard's van. The train was not fitted with continuous brakes as the new system had not been fully introduced. Simple handbrakes were used to apply wooden blocks to the engine, tender and brake van wheels. There was some severe telescoping and evidence of over-running but this accident was not the result of excessive speed. It was reported that all the debris had been cleared, new tracks laid and normal running resumed by 6 pm the same day, a remarkable achievement.

The horrendous wreck of 'The Aberdonian' sleeper in May 1969 was a classic example of a climbing derailment caused by disregarding a permanent speed restriction. The train, which had left Kings Cross at 7.40 the previous evening, consisted of eleven mark 1 vehicles hauled by Deltic locomotive 9011 *Royal Northumberland Fusiliers*. It was a dark, fine night with good visibility enabling landmarks to be easily recognised. The train had observed a speed restriction some miles north of Newcastle but in a lapse of concentration the driver had allowed speed to build up to 82 mph when the train 'hit' the curve at 1.31 am. The maximum permitted speed was then 40 mph.

In the light of day the result of the smash could be seen. Marks on one rail showed the front parcels van was first to leave the track. Miraculously the locomotive remained on the lines and came to rest in the station, 508 yards ahead with the twisted underframe of the van still attached but upside down. The van's bogies were located 300 and 340 yards back and the vehicle had been dragged along on its side until it caught the platform ramp which tossed it up to hit the roof canopy and left it a mangled mess of metal and debris. The train broke into five parts with the second coach standing alone 150 yards behind the diesel, severely damaged but prevented from toppling down a fifteen foot drop by the remains of an old signal box which it had demolished. Its leading bogie was found 250 yards in the rear and the trailing bogie 140 yards, both well to the left of the Down line. Vehicles three and four, still coupled, were flung some 75 feet across to the bank side of the former Wansbeck line and were overtaken by the next four coaches. The sixth coach suffered most damage as the six rear compartments were penetrated by an up-ended length of rail from the siding. It had gone on to its left side at some stage but its wheels remained attached. The last four coaches stayed upright but were all derailed well beyond the line on which they were travelling. Mattresses, bedding, luggage, personal effects, mail, parcels and tons of distorted metal littered the area. A pig travelling in a crate in the leading parcels van was found wandering about but a veterinary surgeon called to the scene declared it had suffered no more than a sore leg!

Breakdown gangs from Gateshead and Edinburgh cleared the lines using their breakdown cranes "with the delicacy of a surgeon's scalpel". New track and ballast were brought in from the Tyne area and both lines were re-opened only twenty-one hours after the accident. Traffic in the meantime was diverted via the Blyth & Tyne though some was re-routed via Carlisle. The damaged coaches, discreetly covered by tarpaulins, were left near the side of the track and were loaded on to 'Sturgeon' wagons by the steam cranes from Gateshead and Doncaster at the end of the month.

The third crash at Morpeth happened in June 1984. In some ways it was almost a copy of the 1969 incident in that both were sleeping car expresses which were taken too fast into a restricted curve, albeit in opposite directions. By this time the speed permitted round the curve had been raised to 50 mph.

The train involved was one from Aberdeen to Kings Cross and consisted of seven modern mark III sleeping cars with a passenger brake van at each end, nine vehicles in all. The accident happened at forty minutes past midnight and subsequent investigations revealed that the speed of the express as it entered the curve was 85-90 mph. The loco 47452, was flung on to its side still facing the direction of travel but lying some sixty feet from the line on which it was travelling. The brake van and the first sleeping car jack-knifed across both tracks. The remainder of the train broke away and careered on what the official report described as "a tangental course across the Down line". The first five of those coaches catapulted on their sides up the bankside, still joined together. The leading vehicle of this group came to rest with one third of its length embedded in an unoccupied bedroom of a bungalow on the hill, 188 metres from the point of derailment. The next one was forced sideways on to the corner of another bungalow, bending the underframe of the sleeping car. The last two vehicles remained upright on the track, detached from the rest of the train though barely. It is interesting to note that ten sheared bogies were all in one confined area.

The force of the sideways fling destroyed the Down main, casting one length of rail over the Up line to lie almost like a handrail up the embankment, its end piercing the greenhouse in a garden about ten metres above. Flying stone ballast broke windows in four houses above the Up line, damaged doors, peppered tiles and landed in the roadway beyond - quite a height and distance! Fortunately, casualties were light in this accident: of the 29 people taken to hospital only the driver and two sleeping car attendants had more serious injuries. Tribute was paid to the excellent design of the sleeping cars whose robustness prevented further casualties.

Many people, the writer included, are interested in what happens after a derailment. At 1.30 pm that same day the Doncaster crane was being manoeuvred into position on the Up line, having been placed ahead of the locomotive at Heaton and allowed to travel on the wrong line for several miles to the site. Using a horizontal beam and slings the crew first edged out the leading van and laid it initially alongside the loco, which, incidentally, was lifted two days later and taken to Gateshead. The Haymarket breakdown train meanwhile waited in the Up platform at Morpeth station. Its loco moved forward and was attached to vehicles 8 and 9. As the class 47 stood on the curve it clearly showed the camber at the spot, over three inches. The sleeping car and parcel van were transferred to the Blyth & Tyne sidings at the other end of the station. Two large road cranes were hired to lift coaches 6 and 7 and place them within reach of the railway cranes.

The Edinburgh crane was initially used to lift short lengths of track and sleepers from a siding and stack them on the adjacent Down platform. These were then laid piece by piece towards the scene of the accident to give crane access on temporary track from the north side. Vehicles 1, 2, 6 and 7 were lifted on to other bogies and left in Morpeth sidings. Coaches 3, 4 and 5 were shielded behind large plastic sheets before the main line was reopened to traffic. The three were laid out wheels-to-roof in the garden of one of the bungalows. Whatever could be salvaged from them was removed and they were finally cut in half and sent off by road. All the others were taken away by rail.

Although these accidents at Morpeth were not on the Blyth & Tyne Branch as such it is relevant to include them because the station was a terminus for branch passenger trains up to 1950 and diverted trains did travel over the line to Benton Quarry, where they rejoined the main line.

Chapter 13

Men of the Branch

THE AUTHOR'S FATHER, James E. Wells, was Station Master at three stations on the Blyth & Tyne Branch - Seaton Delaval (jointly with Seghill), Bedlington and Benton - each one totally different in character. When he was appointed to his first station in 1921, a small one in rural Yorkshire, his salary was £150 a year from which £6 10s 0d (£6.50) was deducted as rent for the station house. The letter he received from the North Eastern Railway stated, "I hope you will do your utmost to give satisfaction both to the travelling public and your employers and be particularly careful in the treatment of the staff under your control; also in the perusal and strict observance of the instructions contained in the Programme and other notices." One of his many interests was staff welfare and he was a regular delegate to national conferences of the Transport Salaried Staffs' Association. On one occasion he supported demands for a better quality uniform, stating, "We are more than disgusted that we have to meet the public in this so-called style. We should have something decent so we don't face people looking like scarecrows!" This provoked a report in one national newspaper headed "We're Scarecrows Station Men Say".

In May 1933 the Blyth News paid tribute to "a great railwayman" - Mr. Thomas Frost, a former Station Master of Blyth, who had died in London the previous week at the age of 87. He was promoted in 1867 when he was about twenty years of age, the youngest official to hold that position. He maintained unbroken service of some 45 years until his retirement in September 1912. After the station was enlarged in 1895 the Company took steps to boost the commercial, shipping and business possibilities and Mr. Frost was authorised to "prepare all the best data available". He did this so well that he was complimented by two top officials of the Company. Mr. Frost read widely and spoke three foreign languages fluently. It could be said he was eccentric about his health, padding his legs and scarcely being on duty without an overcoat and neck-wrap! His father was Station Master at Newsham.

Another report in a Blyth News of 1916 gave details of a driver's long and careful career. Mr. Thomas Scott, of Blyth, who was the oldest engine driver in the service of the North Eastern Railway, retired at the age of 73 years. He served with the old Blyth and Tyne Railway Company and North Eastern Railway Company for 55 years. He had driven locomotives for 48 years, and in the 40 years he was connected with the passenger trains there was never a passenger injured in a train of which he was the driver. He took the first train of coal to the Tyne for shipment from Cambois pit on October 18, 1867, and had the honour of taking the first passenger train from Morpeth into the new station at Manors North. When he started to fire, the passenger trains ran into the first Blyth Station which was opposite the Fox and Hounds Inn in Cowpen Quay.

In the days of steam thousands of schoolboys wanted to become engine drivers, dreaming of being in charge of huge locomotives hurtling along at break-neck speed with important expresses. Many legends have been woven around such exciting thrills and there was a certain aura about being an elite driver. Nevertheless few achieved such fame and the majority were hard-working, genuine men out of the public eye. The following conversation was recorded in 1968 in an interview with the late Andrew ("Ned") Turner then a driver at North Blyth, for the Railway Club at Newsham County Primary School.

"When did you start your railway career?
       In December 1912.
What sort of work did you do then?
       It was customary for the youngest cleaner to call the men up for work during the early hours of the morning.
Did this have a special name?
       You were the 'caller-up'.
Was that your only job?
       Yes it was the only job as I finished at six in the morning. After that I went on cleaning the engines.
What did you do as a cleaner?
       We used to start with the boiler and work down over, cleaning the works, the wheels, tender and everything connected with the engine.
Did everything have to be very clean in those days?
       Oh yes. Yes! If it wasn't the driver was in the office complaining about the dirty state of his engine.
What happened if a complaint was made?
       You had to see the night-shift foreman.
How did you become a fireman?
       Well, I was a bit disappointed when I was asked to go and get my height tested to see if I was the right regulation height.
What do you mean by that, the regulation height?

The regulation height was five feet four.

Do you mean to say you had to be five feet four inches before you could be a fireman?

Oh yes. I was a sixteenth of an inch short for being a fireman!

Only a sixteenth - did they penalize you for that?

They said I would have to wait a while longer. Of course that meant I was losing my turn as a spare fireman.

So, in other words, you had to grow $\frac{1}{16}$" then you would become a fireman?

That's right. I would become a fireman when I measured 5' 4".

When did you become a fireman?

In 1914, during the war. I was transferred to North Blyth.

No doubt you had grown your $\frac{1}{16}$" by then?

Yes, I had.

Will you describe your duties as a fireman?

I would get the oil bottles and take them over to the stores to get the oil for the driver, then I would see that we had detonators and flags, check the water and coal and see that the sandboxes were full before we left the shed.

Would you describe what a detonator is?

If the engine broke down you would take the detonators and put one on the line $\frac{1}{4}$ mile from your engine, one at half a mile and three at three quarters of a mile - then go back to your engine. This was done so that no-one would run into your train from behind.

The detonator is a small explosive charge - is that right? You placed it on the rail and it was exploded if a train went over it.

That's right - it had two lead fingers that you wrapped round the rail and they held it in position on the line until it was detonated or removed.

These are the same things that are used to warn drivers during fog?

Yes, but in that case it is a platelayer who places the detonators on the line.

What are the flags for?

You might get off the rails, anything like that, and block the other line, then you had to run forward with your red flag to stop any oncoming traffic that was going to pass you.

Yes, I see. Now, what would you do on the engine, as a fireman, once you had left the shed?

I would get the pricker down, rake the fire over all the firebox, and put coal on to get plenty of steam up for the driver. It was my job to keep water in the boiler and a hot fire.

How did you train to become a driver?

I used to watch the driver and pick out his good points, then take a turn driving under instruction from the driver, learn routes and attend instruction classes every Sunday morning.

What do you mean by 'learning routes'?

We had to know the routes on which we travelled.

What did you do at the instruction classes?

We used to learn about the engine and how it worked.

Can you tell me what procedure you followed when you reported for work?

We used to look at the 'dockie' to see what engine we had, read the permanent way notices and look for any speed restrictions that were on that section of the line.

In the days of the North Eastern Railway did you always have the same engine?

As far as possible, yes.

The first thing a driver must do is oil his engine and make a check that everything is satisfactory. The main thing is to get your train to its destination in safety and on time. We had to observe all signals in and out and we had to make sure that the fireman did his work properly.

Which passenger duties did you work?

The one that comes into my mind was the Newbiggin to Manors express leaving Newbiggin at 8.45 am and arriving at Manors at 9.35 am.

Can you tell me the class of engine which hauled this train?

It was a G5. (0-4-4T.)

What sort of speed could you attain?

At times we would reach 55 mph. When we were on this duty we used to leave Manors for Morpeth at 11.20 am.

Was this an express or a stopping train?

A stopping train all the way.

Did this include stations like Hepscott?

Yes.

Over the years which classes of engine did you drive?

J21s, J25s, J27s, J39s, J77s and the eight-coupled Q6s.

The J77 was the staiths engine, is that right?

That's right.

The J39 would just be an occasional driving job for you?

Just an occasional one, yes. I remember one J39 that ran away down the Forth Banks, Newcastle, and the fireman and I had to jump off and put wagon brakes down in order to stop at the signals.

Did you also work through to Bellingham?

Yes, we used to take the J21s there.

Do you recall any special incidents when you were a driver.

At Bebside, owing to a mistake by the signalman, I was derailed.

What happened?

I came off all wheels and it needed the steam crane to put us back on.

What was a typical day with a J27 engine?

We would leave Blyth with the van for Shilbottle then take a load of coal to Blyth Power Station, then . . .

Would there be about 400 tons of coal in a train load?

Often more. On another day we might lead coal from Ashington to Blyth.

Can you describe your runs on the Wansbeck line?

We used to leave Blyth with the guard in the van for Morpeth and we used to shunt our train at Morpeth and put it all ready for Bellingham. Sometimes we had loads of guns for military training.

Was there quite a lot of cattle traffic on that line, too?

There was quite a lot - we used to make a special trip with the cattle seeing that they weren't in at Morpeth in time to take them. When we came back (from the normal trip) we had to make a special run so that we could get the cattle back into the fields before night.

How many wagon loads of cattle would there be?

Anywhere between 20 and 30.

Did you take them all in one train load?

Oh, yes.

When was this?

About the year 1959.

You worked for the North Eastern Railway, the London & North Eastern Railway, and British Railways. Did you notice any difference under BR ownership?

Not with the LNER, there was very little difference there but when they were nationalised and called British Railways there did not seem to be the interest in the job that there was previously. Things got gradually worse until I retired in 1961.

The engine with which you were most associated was a J27 -1393, if I remember rightly.

That's right!

This was 13-93 under the LNER and in the renumbering scheme she became 57-97.

That's correct, yes.

And what was the number under BR?

It became 6-57-97.

All the North Eastern region locos had 60,000 added to their old number.

That is correct.

Towards the end of your railway career you drove diesel multiple unit trains. How does one of these compare with driving a steam loco?

Oh, it was much easier. They're a lot cleaner, easier to handle, and you did not get dirty. Even then we still liked the old steam locomotives . . ."

Although it was the practice at one time for a driver to keep his own engine it was not really a practical idea, though it did give him added pride. One driver from South Blyth always had a clean G5, whichever one he had. At the end of each run he was out polishing the engine with his duster even though that wasn't his job. Another Blyth man was known as Auld Jack; always a slow runner but if he was stopped with a goods train at the foot of Bedlington bank he was never known to 'stick'. He just waited for the signal to clear, then opened the regulator, sucked at his clay pipe and sat back until he reached the top.

A retired driver of J27 engines, who had been at Blyth from 1941, stated 65819 was the last engine to work to Rothbury on demolition trains. He was very attached to 'her' and though she had a bad brake he knew exactly what she could do. An engine with good brakes meant you could go "a little bit harder" but even they could let you down occasionally. He recalled he was once taking a set of coal to Percy Main yard with 65838, running tender first, in May 1965. He had tried the sands but found they were not running because the sand was wet and "the pipes were bunged up". He stopped at the top of the bank where the guard pinned down the brakes on three wagons. Normally that would have been sufficient with help from the brake van but on that day drizzle had made the lines very greasy and when he applied the brakes, the tender hand brake as well, the engine just skidded along, pushed by the heavy train. He sounded warning blasts on the whistle then was derailed at the catch points and crashed into the signal box. "I was the only driver to put his tender through Percy Main cabin!" he said.

A signalman, Mr Norman Dalby, worked in Newsham North from 1929 to 1945. He told how his father, grandfather and son had all worked there, too, quite a service record. In his early days he travelled all over to temporary jobs in signal boxes just to keep employed. In his opinion the older generation made it a priority to get to work once they had a secure job. When he earned 55 shillings a week (£2.75) he would have "gone anywhere" for 57s 6d (£2.87½). Most of the drivers and signalmen worked well together and there was a spirit of friendliness which helped them to laugh when things did not go according to plan. He recalled how it normally took eight minutes for a coal train to travel between Hartley and Newsham and the same time from Newsham North to Bebside. Three drivers, one of whom was nicknamed *Bandy*, could do either in six minutes; Isaac was a nine-minute man, but it always used to take Auld Jack seventeen minutes!

In his personal note book another signalman made the following entries:-

Nov. 19th 1912	Blyth Junction Box commenced 8 hours today . . This box was made from 28 shillings to 30 shillings per week from June 21st, being paid all my back money. Champion job.
Dec. 14th 1912	On strike. Strike settled today. Men on strike fined one week's pay. Hard lines. Driver K charged with being drunk caused the strike. C Jones cleared his character not being drunk at the time. The York, Middlesbrough, Stockton centres not coming out on strike caused us to be fined. Fatheads.
March 13th 1913	Engine driver Joe M left for Perth in Australia. Good old Joe. Joe B removed to Percy Main to start as driver on the bombs.

It is perhaps worth recording that a certain signalman whose Christian names were Edward Stanley had two sons. The first one was called after his father, Edward Stanley - the younger one was Stanley Edward.

Stories once told often change when they are repeated. One location is substituted for another, *characters* are different and the details vary. Nevertheless, this is said to be the original version of one tale, though the names may be different. An afternoon passenger train from Manors, hauled by a G5 class 0-4-4 tank loco, came down the bank from Seghill to Seaton Delaval but on a greasy rail the engine and three of the coaches overshot the platform and passed under the bridge. The guard opened the door of the rear van and apologised to the porter, "Sorry about that, Jackie, we'll have to shunt back." Without a smile the porter laconically remarked, "Divvent worry, Billy, we'll just shift the station!"

The staff at Seaton Delaval were always very understanding towards a cheery young man who in the early 1940s walked past the station twice a day, giving a little kick to posts, gates and big stones saying to each one "Half past six". When children asked his name or any other question, the answer was always "Half past six". Then, with a wave, he continued his walk.

In his book "By Rail to Victory - the Story of the LNER in Wartime", Norman Crump gave credit to the men who bravely faced so many dangers the night New Bridge Street goods station was bombed. Looking back they must have recalled some amusing moments . . .

Station staff at Benton circa 1920. (G E Charlton collection)

"In the basement there were stabled a number of lorries and mechanical horses. Mr T Robson and 'Frankie' Mackenzie went down to try to get them out. The only way out was through a tunnel under New Bridge Street, Air sucked through this was blowing like a gale, and the tunnel was full of smoke. Water from the firemens' hoses was by this time pouring into the basement, together with flour from the blazing chutes. In this inferno Robson and Mackenzie, with Mr Dale and one or two others, got to work. They rescued a number of vehicles by either persuading their engines to start or in extreme cases pushing them out. Eventually Frankie Mackenzie disappeared, and Robson thought he was lost. A short time afterwards a white ghost staggered towards him out of the smoke. It was Frankie, completely enveloped in a paste of flour and water . . . Meanwhile salvage work continued on the street level. It was perilous work, for the fire was raging up above, and all sorts of things were pouring down through holes in the ceiling. One man would be suddenly smothered in a cascade of hot treacle. Then would come a shower of warm water, mixed up with linseed and flour. Another man was actually deluged with *liver salts!* Nevertheless, goods were salvaged wherever possible. One gang got away three or four wagons intact. Another gang found a wagon-load of tobacco intact between burning trucks on either side. The tobacco was unloaded and rescued. In another part of the goods station cases of bacon and margarine were recovered. Much indeed was lost, but thanks to the devotion of the men on duty there, much was saved . . ."

After the General Strike of 1926 the LNER organised a dinner in the County Hotel, Newcastle, for the volunteers who had helped to run the railway. The menu on that occasion is printed on the next page.

Toasts were proposed to The King,
The London & North Eastern Railway
Company,
and The Volunteers.

These were followed by a programme of music and entertainment.

There is no doubt that real, genuine railwaymen were the salt of the earth, a race apart. It is true their ranks contained many *characters* but their job was to run the railway and this they did, very well. Other important things to them - like football pools - had their attention, too, witness a note accidentally filed away with old circulars:-

George
Bob reckons your last week's Coupon was void owing to you having taken the same team twice. Have a word with him if possible.
Harry.

Perhaps they won the following week. We'll never know!

Menu.

◆

Soup.

Thick a la Superheat.

Clear Neck Oil.

Fish.

For Points and Signals.

Joints.

Roast Beef a la Shunters and Stokers' Pudding.

Lamb ('Tender as a Porter).

Tetties (Hard or Soft).   Boiled Detonators.

Electro Pneumatic Cabbage.

Sweets.

Boiled Strawberry Sweat Rags.

Ticket Collectors' Delight with Palm Oil.

Carlisle Cheese and Biscuits.

Rabbit Meat.

Signal Box Coffee.

Chapter 14

The Tyneside Metro

WHEN ELECTRIC TRAINS were introduced on the Newcastle to Tynemouth section of the Blyth & Tyne Branch in 1904 they were the first in Britain - but the North East of England has frequently produced world-beating ideas and technology, not only for railways but in shipbuilding, mining and engineering. The opening of the initial section of the Tyneside Metro in 1980, the first rapid light transit system in the United Kingdom and the backbone of an integrated transport system, was yet another success story for the original Blyth & Tyne Railway route from Newcastle to the coast via Benton.

Before this golden egg hatched, however, there was a long incubation period during which in-depth studies were made of the whole transport system on Tyneside. On the railway side, Newcastle had always been one of the largest and most important centres in the country but its stations at Central and Manors were not conveniently placed, being on the edge of the city centre. When industry was at its most productive state in the area a great deal of heavy road traffic was always in evidence. Thousands of people travelled to work or to shop in the city, a large proportion using buses. At that time, too, the main trunk road (the A1) passed right through Newcastle, Gateshead, and their suburbs. There was over ten miles of continuous built-up area with traffic often reduced to a crawl, all this compounded by the rapidly growing number of car owners. Obviously this was a major problem which, with the need for increased mobility, could only get worse. The solution had to be bold, ruthless but imaginative.

In the late 1960s a partnership of Government, local authorities and transport operators produced the Tyne-Wear Plan which proposed "significant investment in a public transport system with its own right of way based on the current railway with renewal and upgrading of lines and stations and improvements in central area accessibility." The Tyneside Passenger Transport Authority, formed about that time, adopted the Plan and took steps to secure the necessary finance and legislation to permit the Metro system to develop. The Tyne & Wear

Council, formed in 1974, also gave the project total support. In essence, the scheme was to take over certain existing railway routes belonging to British Rail, then to extend these underground and create stations at strategic points in the city, and across the river. New interchange centres would be built where buses would start or terminate their journeys and passengers would travel out to, or in from, these centres using a Transfare ticket. This would take hundreds of buses away from town centres, while the provision of car parking facilities at stations would encourage motorists to use the new trains. The Tyneside Metropolitan Railway Act of 1973 gave Parliamentary approval for the project and major construction started in 1974.

British Rail stations at Jesmond, West Jesmond, South Gosforth, Longbenton and Benton were closed to passengers on 23 January 1978 and a bus service between them was substituted. Backworth had already been closed in June 1977. West Monkseaton, Monkseaton, Whitley Bay and Cullercoats followed on 10 September 1979. The southern end of Tynemouth remained open for diesel trains to and from Newcastle via Wallsend until that section was closed on 11 August 1980 prior to the extension of the Metro between Tynemouth and St. James, which was opened in November 1982. Stations such as Benton, Monkseaton and Whitley Bay were retained to keep as much as possible of their original character whereas the new ones at the interchanges or underground were designed to be attractive yet functional, easily maintained and reasonably vandal-proof.

Principal features involved in creating the Metro system were some three miles of tunnelling, new bridges (notably the Queen Elizabeth bridge across the River Tyne), raising the height of road bridges, installing masts and overhead wires, building new stations or adapting existing ones, altering platform levels, plus a complete re-signalling. In Newcastle alone new underground stations were built at Central, Haymarket, Monument, St. James and Manors.

The prototype cars, 4001 and 4002, were delivered to a test track at Middle Engine Lane, near Murton (grid reference NZ 323693) in 1975 where they were subjected to considerable trials and used for basic crew training. Some modifications which were found necessary were incorporated into the production models, numbered 4003 to 4090, all of which were built by Metro Cammell Ltd of Birmingham. Two Hong Kong Metro cars were also tested there in February and March 1978. Over 11,000 people visited the test centre before it closed in 1980. The original vehicles remained in store at Gosforth Depot as they were not compatible with other stock but after some alterations were carried out by Messrs Hunslet of Leeds they joined the fleet in July 1987. Initially there was some controversy as to whether the Metrocars were trains or trams - so would they be driven by engine drivers or bus drivers? It seems obvious that as they run on *railway* lines they are *trains*.

The coaches consist of lightweight, twin articulated units running on three bogies, designed to carry large numbers of passengers over short distances. Each two-section vehicle is 27.8 metres in length with seating for 84 passengers, though if necessary up to 188 people standing can also be carried. There are four wide passenger doors on each side to allow for speedy boarding and alighting. The doors are opened by push buttons but closed by the driver after a warning horn has been sounded. Current at 1500 volts DC is collected from overhead wires by means of pantographs and drives the two axles of each outer bogie through right angle drive units. Maximum speed is 80 km/hour, i.e. 50 mph. In normal circumstances not more than two Metrocars are coupled together but at night time and on quiet Sundays they run singly. Their colour scheme, which matched that of the buses originally, is officially given as Newcastle cadmium yellow for the lower panel, separated by a stripe of French blue from brilliant white: the roof is storm grey and the front or rear windows matt black. These trains are operated by one person only but drivers and other staff are in radio contact with the Central Control at Gosforth.

When first introduced, the Metro trains carried the logos of the Passenger Transport Executive and Tyne and Wear County Council, representing the policy of public transport integration north and south of the River Tyne. Following the demise of Metropolitan County Councils and the deregulation of buses, Metro was given its own identity. A large, black 'M' like those used to denote stations, is now on the end of each coach with a smaller one on the train sides ahead of the words 'Tyne & Wear Metro'. Their new logo, angular 'TW' letters flowing together, also appears on each vehicle.

Stations are not manned though are visited very regularly by staff. Passengers have to obtain the necessary ticket from a machine unless they have a Travelcard or Transfare ticket. Each station on the system is listed with a code letter or number alongside. When the appropriate button is pressed the required fare is visually displayed. The machine accepts coins and gives change but if it has no change this, too, is shown. Children travel for a nominal fare (still 10p to any destination in 1989) but anyone who presses the Reduced Fare button is immediately challenged visually and by a two-note audible warning to check whether he or she is entitled to a cheap ticket. Return tickets to stations in Newcastle were introduced early in 1988 but withdrawn the following November. Access to platforms was gained by inserting a valid ticket at one of the entry turnstiles. A ticket, for example, that had been used previously would be rejected but towards the end of 1988 passengers could walk straight through the barriers without inserting their ticket. The purpose of this was to speed up entry to platforms. Each station had a wide barrier for use by people in wheelchairs or with push chairs. During 1989 most barriers were removed. To combat the small minority who board trains without paying and thereby abuse the system, teams of travelling inspectors working in pairs or in fours check tickets during journeys and can impose fixed penalties or recommend court action against offenders.

The safe operation of the Metro is the responsibility of System Control. Each running line, signal, level crossing, siding, set of points and terminal bays is shown on a large display panel. Occupied sections of line are illuminated in red; white shows when a section of track has been made available for a particular train. Each train is indicated by an identification number which moves as the train progresses. Route setting is initiated by each driver who sets his route code on thumbwheels in his cab before each trip. Once he presses the 'Ready to Start' button at a terminus this information is fed to route setting equipment at South Gosforth which, as the train progresses, clears automatic signals, changes points and alters destination indicators at those stations which have them. At junctions trains are passed through on the first there first served principle. Those requiring conflicting movements are held back until the one ahead is clear, then the route and signals are reset automatically. The controller can, of course, override the system to allow for unscheduled operations or to restore trains to time by giving them priority. He can set routes, or change points and signals, in the modern conventional manner all of which are interlocked for safety.

The first section of the Metro, between Haymarket and Tynemouth via Benton, was opened to the public on 11 August 1980. In September of the following year a presentation was made to the 10 millionth passenger! There followed extensions of the system from

A Tyneside Metro train crossing over the Blyth & Tyne route east of Benton station in 1984. (J A Wells)

In 1989 two Metrocars were painted in the liveries of two local railways to celebrate their 150th anniversaries. Cars 4044, named Director, *and 4051,* Times, *are seen at Benton. (J A Wells)*

Haymarket to Heworth (November 1981):
Tynemouth to St. James (November 1982):
and   South Shields to Bankfoot,
thus completing the initial scheme, in March 1984. Reference to the
map on page 158 will reveal there are now four routes which are:-
Pelaw to St. James, via Benton and Tynemouth (yellow)
Pelaw to Benton (red)
South Shields to Bank Foot, the former Ponteland Branch
(green)
North Shields to St. James (blue)
  Destination panels on the trains have the appropriate coloured
background as do some station indicators. Maps in stations also use
corresponding colours. A ten minute service in both directions is
scheduled during the working day on each of these routes. Together
they provide a train every three minutes between South Gosforth and
Pelaw, and every five minutes between North Shields and St. James.
By the end of March 1984 the Metro had already carried 115 million
passengers: five years later it was over one million a week.
  As this book relates particularly to the Blyth & Tyne Branch it is
appropriate to look more closely at the stations between Jesmond
and Tynemouth.
  The line through Central, Monument and Haymarket surfaces just
beyond Jesmond Metro station where it joins the former Blyth & Tyne
route. A line through the old station has been retained so that empty
trains between St. James and the car sheds via Manors can use it as
a short cut and save going right round the system via Tynemouth. The
original Blyth & Tyne station, cleaned up, survives as a restaurant with
a former Great Northern Railway dining car providing extra accommodation and a new structure in the shape of a signal box serving the
same purpose. At West Jesmond the buildings have been retained
though the platform awnings have been removed and a new
footbridge can be used instead of the subway. Ilford Road is a new
station with the typical Metro shelter. It is near the site of the former
Moor Edge station, opened by the Blyth & Tyne Railway Company
to cater for race traffic but closed after the new race course was
opened at Gosforth Park. The next station can be seen just along the
track.
  The old coach body mentioned on page 57 is still there on the
approach to South Gosforth but considerably reduced in size. As this
station was chosen to be the Control Centre for the whole Metro area,

the former B & T R buildings were demolished. The modern structure erected in their place has totally changed the appearance of this once attractive station. A standard Metro shelter has replaced the old waiting room on the former Up platform. A run-in siding was laid at a later date mainly for trains which were being taken out of service. The North Eastern footbridge is still in use, adding a touch of colour in its bright red livery. Once under the road bridge the tracks divide as before, those on the left going to Bank Foot, and on the right to Tynemouth. The triangular junction is retained and the former electric car sheds continue in use for stabling, cleaning, painting and repairing Metro stock. The Lucozade factory, having stood empty for some time, was finally demolished early in 1988 to make way for housing development.

Little alteration was needed at Longbenton although a new footbridge with ramps was built especially for disabled people. One of the rail-bus-car interchange centres was constructed at Four Lane Ends where the original Blyth & Tyne station, Longbenton, once stood.

On the Branch certain alterations were made to the trackwork and this was in evidence at Benton. The triple junction was simplified and subsequently changed again during track repairs in November 1984, when the junction to the former south west curve was modified into a facing crossover and simple point. The former north west curve became two shortened sidings to hold trains terminating at Benton. British Rail retained control of the south east curve for a connecting line to Earsdon, Seghill and beyond which, after an initial section of double track from Benton Quarry to allow trains to pass, is a single line running alongside the double track of the Metro. It was necessary to build a flyover to enable Metro trains cross the British Rail lines.

The next station after Benton used to be Backworth but the new Metro station was built much nearer the village of Shiremoor and carries that name. It is only a short distance from where the Blyth & Tyne Railway built Hotspur Place. As it was a long stretch between Benton and Shiremoor another station, Palmersville, was constructed between them in 1986. It stands on the site of Benton Square which was opened by the North Eastern Railway on 1 July 1909 and closed in September 1915. *Ilford Road* near Moor Edge, *Four Lane Ends* on the site of the original Longbenton, *Palmersville* where Benton Square stood and *Shiremoor* only yards from Hotspur Place - it seems the wheel has turned full circle!

West Monkseaton still has one of the original LNER waiting rooms from 1933 and a wooden platform. At Monkseaton the various buildings of the main block on the Down side are intact, even a seaside scene in coloured glass has been added to one of the vertical sections at the end of the roof awning. Whitley Bay and Cullercoats have had the covered portion of the station reduced in size; the latter also retains the covered footbridge. When these three stations were last painted the colours used were reminiscent of those seen in North Eastern days, a nostalgic touch. It is interesting to note that a North Eastern Railway lower quadrant signal survived in use at Whitley Bay until 1979.

Tynemouth was always a well kept station but it was really too big for Metro's requirements. The first proposal was to construct a much smaller one at the north end but public opinion forced a rethink. The renowned Victorian building must stay! After numerous meetings as to its future it was finally decided in 1985 that extensive renovations would be carried out to the station buildings and to the roof with its decorative supports, a slow but worthwhile process using Community Service Volunteers. In addition, the Saturday flea markets would continue, retail outlets would be made in the station and on adjoining land; there would be a restaurant, community and sports provision, training and workspace facilities and offices, and a Fire & Safety Museum. All in all this is proving to be an ambitious redevelopment programme but phase 1 is already complete.

On the north side of the river, Metro has maintenance depots at New Bridge Street, Benton and North Shields. The five Works Locomotives, numbered WL1 - WL5, are all 0-6-0 diesel electrics built by Brush, based on a design for the Nigerian Railways. They are powered by 427 hp Rolls Royce engines and capable of speeds up to 30 mph. Three shunting locomotives were brought from NEI Parsons when the rail network was closed at their Heaton Works.

Twelve new bogie flat wagons, supplied in the autumn of 1977 were modified in different ways to provide cable carriers, mobile cranes, scaffolding wagons and rail loaders. Other wagons obtained second hand from British Rail, NEI Parsons, or other sources, included some 'Walrus' ballast hoppers, bogie bolsters, 4-wheeled 'medfits', an 80-ton 'Weltrol' and two brake vans used for travelling and mess accommodation for engineering staff. Other vehicles, such as 'Lowmacs', were hired from BR in the early days to carry rail mounted Poclain excavators for mast erection. Two low-height spoil wagons, permanently coupled and having standard Metrocar BSI autocouplers on the outer ends, in addition to normal buffers and drawhooks were purchased from Procor in 1986, plus two Geismar Rail Loaders.

1989 saw the 150th Anniversary of two local railways and to celebrate these auspicious occasions two Metrocars were painted in the colours of those companies. Number 4051 was transformed when it appeared in the rich, claret livery of the Newcastle & North Shields Railway (the world's first suburban railway), beautifully lined out in gold and bearing the name TIMES. Its partner, number 4044, was turned out in the bright yellow of the Brandling Junction Railway which connected Gateshead, South Shields and Sunderland. It was named DIRECTOR after one of the original carriages on that line. The pair has continued in regular passenger services between Pelaw and St. James or Pelaw and Benton. Significantly, this train passes along the section between Jesmond and Monkseaton (formerly Whitley) which was opened by the Blyth & Tyne Railway in 1864, hence it was 125 years old in 1989.

One final link with the Blyth & Tyne Branch which must be mentioned was the running of infrequent freight trains (a maximum of 10 per month in 1988) by British Rail over Metro tracks. Under this agreement the rail connection with Rowntree's factory at Coxlodge and the ICI explosives plant at Callerton was maintained. Short Railfreight trains travelled via Benton Quarry and the south west curve, through Benton, Four Lane Ends and Longbenton stations then along the former Ponteland branch, with a return working in the opposite direction. Messrs Rowntrees stopped using the rail transport early in 1987 and the last run to Callerton was in April 1989.

A quotation attributed to Emerson stated, "If a man write a better book, preach a better sermon, or make a better mousetrap than his neighbour, tho' he build his house in the woods, the world will make a beaten path to his door." Thousands of people from the British Isles and overseas have come to the North East again to see the organisation and operation of the Metro. Many from abroad have already shown specific interest in the British-built Metro-cars, signalling, power supply and civil engineering works. The Metro is undoubtedly a popular system - clean, efficient and well supported. The people it serves are very proud of it, and with justification.

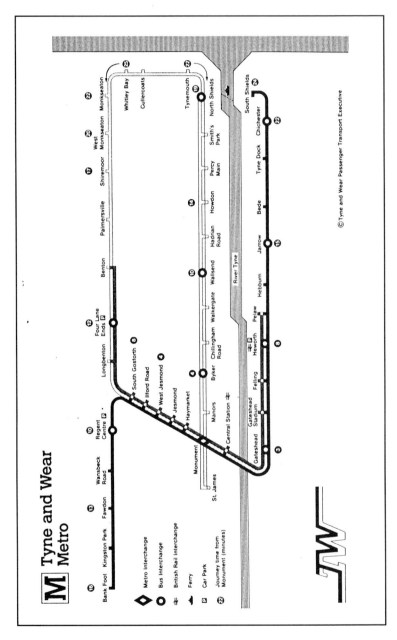

Fig. 17

Chapter 15

A Hundred Years On
- and beyond

IT WAS TOWARDS the end of January 1874 that terms of amalgamation were agreed between the North Eastern Railway and the Blyth & Tyne Railway Company, but as this was not legalised until 7 August of that year it was 1875 before changes were felt. There followed a long period of progress and expansion from which the NER reaped rich rewards. A hundred years later, the year in which celebrations were held to mark the 150th Anniversary of the Stockton & Darlington Railway (the world's first public railway) it was a different story with the Branch reflecting the social and economic changes of the time. In the wake of the Beeching Report, passenger trains from stations north of Backworth were withdrawn on 2 November 1964 and goods traffic at various dates before or after that. Numerous collieries were closed and the reduction in coal traffic through Blyth resulted in staiths being demolished and sidings taken up. Later, the advent of the Metro removed the Newcastle to Tynemouth section of the Branch from British Rail.

It could be said that in 1989 the Blyth & Tyne Branch was a mere shadow of its former self. At Newcastle Central the platforms at the east end (used in the past by trains to and from the coast) have been made into a car-parking area. What was at one time the world's largest diamond crossing has been steadily reduced in size though most recent changes to the track layout have enabled two extra through platforms to be built on the south side of the station.

Demolition of the platform awnings at Manors began in 1979, leaving vandalised dereliction before the north side of the station was razed to make way for major road schemes. The former coal yard, the warehouse and the sidings at New Bridge Street have all gone. Further down the line, the length between Percy Main and Earsdon was made into single track. Its final use was for conveying fuel oil to Cambois motive power depot but it was closed completely in July 1983 and the track was lifted in September 1984.

The remainder of the Branch is now single line apart from Bedlington to Ashington and Cambois. Stations at Seghill, Seaton Delaval and Hartley have been demolished though the station house at the latter (a Blyth & Tyne Railway building) remains as a private dwelling. When one of the tracks was removed at Hartley the opportunity was taken to ease the tight curve through the platforms. Another Blyth & Tyne house, occupied by the former Station Master for several years after the station's closure, is still at Newsham. Again all the sidings but one have been removed though a connection which led to the site of the former Isabella Colliery sidings and Bates loading terminal was retained. Where Blyth station stood there is now a Presto supermarket and car park. A new hospital, opened in 1987, covers the former goods yard area. Bebside boasted the last set of level crossing gates on the Branch until they were converted to barriers about 1984.

At Bedlington part of the station, the platform, both signal boxes and the former station house are still there. Buildings on the platform are being used by the Permanent Way Department. Under the old system, when trains were required to change direction at the junction, locomotives ran round their train between the two signal boxes. Now, because of the length of coal trains, it is necessary to use the Furnace Way sidings for that purpose. North Seaton station is no longer there but the signal box continues to control the level crossing. The site of Ashington station can be recognised from the remains of the platforms near the hospital. Once under the road bridge the tracks divide, one route goes to Butterwell opencast and the other to Lynemouth. The line to Newbiggin has disappeared.

Nothing is left of the buildings at Choppington but at Hepscott the former station has been an attractive, private house for over twenty years. In spite of its small size, Hepscott can claim the distinction of having a main-line steam locomotive there for several months from the autumn of 1988. 'Black 5' number 44767, named *George Stephenson* in 1975, and normally based on the North Yorkshire Moors Railway, was brought in by road so that its owner, Ian Story, could carry out essential repairs at his engineering workshops alongside the line. From Morpeth traffic can now pass on to the Blyth & Tyne Branch direct from the north and the south main lines. The cattle mart, which provided so much livestock for transport by rail in past years, has been flattened and replaced by houses.

Only a few signal boxes are left to echo the Absolute Block System on the Branch. Newsham South - very much smaller than its former partner Newsham North, and now called simply Newsham - works to Benton in one direction and Bedlington South in the other. Bedlington and North Seaton have been mentioned: the others are Ashington, Marcheys House, Winning and Freemans Crossing which controls entry to Blyth power station and the west staiths. All the rest have been uncompromisingly destroyed. Level crossing barriers are now worked either from a signal box, with the aid of television cameras if necessary, or by train-operated treadles.

Thus things change and progress. Nothing remains the same. What is no longer required is discarded unless it is preserved elsewhere as a reminder of bygone days.

Although it may appear that everything is doom and gloom there is in fact an air of optimism following British Rail's investment in modern locomotives, rolling stock and equipment. Merry-go-round trains continue to ferry full loads to Blyth power station, some from the Durham coalfield. The class 56 diesel locomotives can handle more than twice the load of a J27. Currently between 80,000 and 100,000 tonnes of coal are being moved on the Branch each week. Under the three-letter coding for computer purposes most of these coal wagons are classified as HAA (Hopper, type A, Air-braked). Each can carry 32 tonnes and the normal train length is now 36. As a rule they are all braked from the engine but it is accepted that up to three wagons in any one train can travel with the brakes temporarily inoperable. It is essential that the brakes on the last three vehicles do work properly, then in the event of a divided train both parts would stop automatically. There are still some of the old $24\frac{1}{2}$-ton capacity steel mineral hoppers about but these are being phased out and will be a thing of the past on the Blyth & Tyne.

The west staiths at Blyth were used for loading coal into ships for transfer to the south of England, also for export to various parts of Europe. For many years there has been a regular trade with Ireland though a recent innovation was an agreement with Messrs Cawoods for British Rail to transport the coal in open containers to Ellesmere Port, Cheshire, prior to being transferred to container ships. Five trains a week, of 42 four-wheeled wagons carrying 21 tonnes each, are taken from Lynemouth as far as York by a class 56 based at Cambois. The majority of household coal from Lynemouth (which is connected to Ellington Colliery) is now carried by rail. Following the reduction of traffic the wooden staiths at 'The West', the last in the country in regular use, were taken out of commission on 31 December 1989. Perhaps they should be preserved as a reminder of the town's importance as a coal-handling port.

During 1989 the decision was taken to reinstate and modernise the Bates loading terminal at Blyth to handle up to eight full loads a day. Track will be relaid from Newsham along the Isabella Colliery line to a new unloading and storage complex beside the river. It is anticipated this will be in use at the end of 1990, meanwhile the single siding at Newsham has already been made into a loop to provide a run-around facility for trains from beyond Bedlington. Signals, too, have been erected.

The closure of Ashington in March 1988 left Ellington as the only colliery in Northumberland producing coal, much of which is mined from three miles or more out under the North Sea. Forty years ago there were some sixty pits in the area. For opencast coal from Butterwell it was the practice to take empty trains in via Ashington but for full loads to leave near Pegswood and travel south on the main line before joining the Blyth & Tyne route north of Morpeth. A new system of two-way signalling was installed in 1988 which enables trains for Cambois to leave by Ashington and use the shorter route to Blyth, thus saving the reversal at Bedlington. Train loads for destinations further south (to ICI Wilton, for example) continue to use the main line.

Locos for scrap! A string of rebuilt B16 class 4-6-0s await their fate at the yard of Hughes Bolckow, Blyth. (J Nicholson)

The transfer of fuel oil for Cambois depot from rail to road leaves alumina and aluminium as the only other traffic. From storage silos alongside the River Blyth, alumina is conveyed to the Lynemouth smelter in covered hopper wagons with loads averaging 800 tonnes. These are unfitted, loose-coupled trains, though they will be up-graded in the future from class 9 freights.

Some alumina is now taken from Blyth to Millerhill, Edinburgh, in fully-braked trains of 450-500 tonnes. This traffic is then taken forward to Fort William. These vehicles, in blue livery, are privately-owned and marked ALCAN.

Aluminium ingots used to be sent by road to the Freightliner depot at Follingsby, south of the Tyne but following the closure of that depot Freightliner wagons are now taken over the Branch to be loaded at Lynemouth in Alcan's private sidings. Originally these trains were taken by a Cambois crew to Tyne Yard for transfer to Tees Yard, then on to Cardiff, but a re-organisation has given this working to Thornaby. Long *Cargo-Waggons* and VTG vans are used to carry exports of rolls of aluminium to France, Germany and Italy.

The motive power depot at Cambois shares with South Dock the handling of all coal sent by rail from Northumberland and Durham. They have a pool of 24 class 56 locomotives of which, say, 17 would be available at any one time, with six working from Cambois and eleven from South Dock, depending on traffic. Various problems in the Yorkshire coalfield, for example, meant that requirements of coal from the North East to Yorkshire power stations were doubled - with only 48 hours notice! There were two class 37s based at Cambois for metal traffic but now only one, plus two or three 08 shunters. The depot has been upgraded to maintain diesels for 'A' and 'B' examinations. Category 'C'. 'D' and 'F' overhauls are carried out at Toton.

Maintenance of BR wagons for such things as springs, buffers, axle-boxes and wheels is carried out in the open at Cambois by a team of fitters. Privately-owned vehicles are also serviced there by an independent firm. BR stock requiring major overhaul is sent to Knottingly now that Shildon is closed.

Cambois is linked to the national computer system known as TOPS (Total Operations Processing System) which stores details of every engine and wagon and their last location. If a vehicle is in transit the computer can give such information as its load, destination, arrival time, and where it has to go next. It is not used so much for coal wagons. It is because of this system that the codes of wagons, vans, departmental and service vehicles have been changed to three letters.

Another programme, called MAIDENS (Micro AIded Diagram ENactmentS) has been tried successfully at Cambois and a similar one has been produced for other depots. The computer works out how long it takes for a train to be assembled, travelling time for the loco to reach its train, how long it would take to travel to various destinations depending on the load and type of loco diagrammed, arrival and departure times, how much of the driver's shift remains after each specific duty, and the percentage of the driver's time usefully employed. Its purpose is to help staff plan duty rosters so as to make the most efficient use of time. At the beginning of his shift a driver is given a print-out showing details of what he is required to do over the next seven, eight or nine hours.

In the realm of railway preservation several major items which were used on the Blyth & Tyne Branch, or which typify the locomotives, coaches and wagons therefrom, survive in several locations. Members of the North Eastern Locomotive Preservation Group (NELPG) have successfully restored a P3 (LNER/BR J27), at T2 (LNER/BR Q6) a J72 and an LNER/BR K1, all of which are based on the North Yorkshire Moors Railway. The K1 finished its working life at North Blyth.

At Beamish museum a North Eastern Railway country station has been created. There is a working NER class C 0-6-0, number 876 (BR65033) in green livery; also the former Percy Main tool van, 92189; a bogie stores van, snowplough (NER number 20), several mineral wagons and a brake van. The LNER and, later, British Railways sold to Ashington Colliery some former NER coaches, between 1946 and 1955. They were for internal use on the colliery railway system. Four of these are being fully restored at Beamish; a fifth, unfortunately, was damaged by fire.

One of the features at Monkwearmouth Station Museum, Sunderland, is a typical North Eastern booking office.

An exciting project is under way at Middle Engine Lane where the former Metro workshop has been converted to house railway artifacts in the Stephenson Museum. Principal exhibits include George Stephenson's first Killingworth locomotive and the cab-shell from a Blyth & Tyne engine. A North Eastern Railway electric parcels van is being carefully restored and will be in the smart red and cream original livery. A major event in 1989 was the arrival of LNER A4

End of the line for the Avenue branch. The well-painted level crossing gates have not yet been removed but the signal box - still bearing its name Avenue Crossing - *has been gutted. (collection of the late Jim Scott)*

number 2509 *Silver Link* as a static exhibit for three years. To be correct this locomotive is actually *Bittern* of the same class (now privately owned) which was given a cosmetic restoration to appear as part of the 1988 celebrations of MALLARD's world record-breaking run of 3 July 1938 (126 mph). *Silver Link* in grey (itself a record holder and first of the A4 class), *Mallard* in garter blue, and *Union of South Africa* in Brunswick green showed three of the liveries carried by this famous class of locomotive since it was introduced in 1935.

The NER P3 number 2392 (LNER J27 No. 5894: BR No. 65894) was also at Middle Engine Lane undergoing repairs in the workshops at the end of 1989. It appeared in steam on special occasions before being 'shopped'. Already a two mile stretch of railway has been laid from the Museum to Percy Main along the former Blyth & Tyne route. The terminus at Percy Main is on the site of the original station of 1840, beside the present Metro station of the same name. Passenger trains will be running in 1990 possibly using the unique Kitson long-boilered pannier tank engine and three ex LNER coaches that ran on suburban services to and from Kings Cross. Other locomotives will be used when available.

After discussion in recent months between interested parties, a feasibility study is to consider an extension of the line from Middle Engine Lane to Earsdon and through to Woodhorn, using steam locomotives at times. This may be a very attractive proposal, particularly to railway enthusiasts, but its practicality is open to question.

A small Railway Museum specialising in items from the Blyth & Tyne Branch was opened at Princess Louise Middle School, Blyth in 1977 and remained for eleven years. In recent months a start has been made on a Mining Museum at the former Woodhorn Colliery, near Ashington. Woodhorn was one of the collieries connected to the Branch and if the above scheme ever does materialise it would become the northern terminus, according to press reports.

The former Marsden & Whitburn Colliery branch of the Harton Coal Company operated a passenger train service for miners living in South Shields. Members of the public were permitted to use the train which was always affectionately known in the area as *The Marsden Rattler*. The line is no longer there but the name is perpetuated in a sea-front restaurant made from three bogie coaches. Incorporated into the main building, from Manors station, are some columns, roof-girders and awnings from platform 1, together with some door and window surrounds. Another notable feature from the same station is the clock with a typical Edwardian cupola - altogether a happy reminder of a bygone age.

The Blyth & Tyne sidings at Morpeth had considerable use during part of 1988 and throughout 1989 in connection with the electrification of the east coast main line. Renewing of track, ballasting, tamping, putting in bases and erecting masts and cables, in a formidable programme, brought an interesting variety of works trains. The station roof had to be moved back by a metre, in one piece, in a delicate operation so that it would not interfere with pantographs on electric locomotives. The former Blyth & Tyne station, part of which had been rented for ten years by Greens, the Agricultural Merchants, was vacated at the end of 1988. "Could this building have been used in 1881 by the Government authorities for prison purposes?" This question is asked by A H Tweddle in his *Town Trail for Morpethians, Number 8.* He notes "in that year the Morpeth Herald informs us that the large stone building near the Station was being taken out of use by the Governor of Morpeth Gaol, for all their prisoners and warders were being transferred to the Newcastle Gaol." Messrs Green moved into custom-built premises between the old station and the goods shed. The facade of their new building is of stone and its windows closely follow the style of the Blyth & Tyne station. Even the porch has been incorporated as a design feature, a thoughtful idea.

This, then is the unique Blyth & Tyne Branch as we enter the nineties. In spite of its small size it has had a colourful and varied history and has been the centre of innovations eagerly copied by others. Perhaps the judicious pruning of recent years has created new growth which will bear more fruit in the future. Somehow the enterprise and enthusiasm - indeed the *spirit* of the Branch - still persists. For the sake of generations of Railwaymen let us hope this will continue for many years to come.

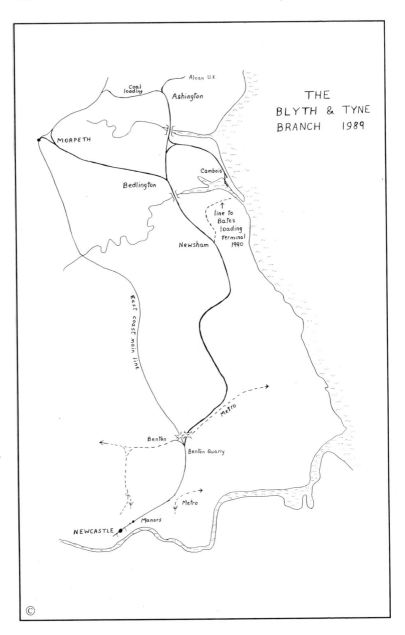

Fig. 18

Track Diagrams

APART FROM THE large, framed layout plans which were a feature of all signal boxes, the railways produced numerous smaller track diagrams for use by various departments. These were usually referred to as *white prints* and showed not only the arrangement of tracks but also the number of each signal, point, etc. in the appropriate signal box plus the length and capacity of sidings or other relevant material as required. They were issued, for example, when alterations were made to platforms, extra tracks laid, sidings lengthened, for resignalling purposes or when buildings were to be extended. Many of these survive and the following pages show most of the locations on the Blyth & Tyne Branch as they were at some time in their history. The plans are not drawn to scale.

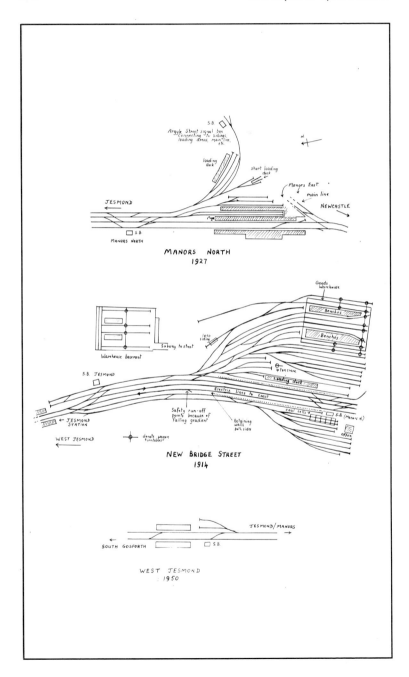

S.B.

Argyle Street signal box
connecting "to sidings,
loading areas, main line,
etc.

N

loading
dock

short loading
dock

Manors East

main line

JESMOND

NEWCASTLE

S.B.

MANORS NORTH

MANORS NORTH
1927

Goods
Warehouse

Benches

Benches

Subway to street

lgto
siding

fan crane

Warehouse basement

S.B. JESMOND

Loading dock

Electric lines to coast

JESMOND
STATION

Safety run-off
points because of
falling gradient

coal cells

S.B. (Manors N)

Retaining
walls
both sides

office

WEST JESMOND

denote wagon
turntables

NEW BRIDGE STREET
1914

JESMOND/MANORS

SOUTH GOSFORTH

S.B.

WEST JESMOND
1950

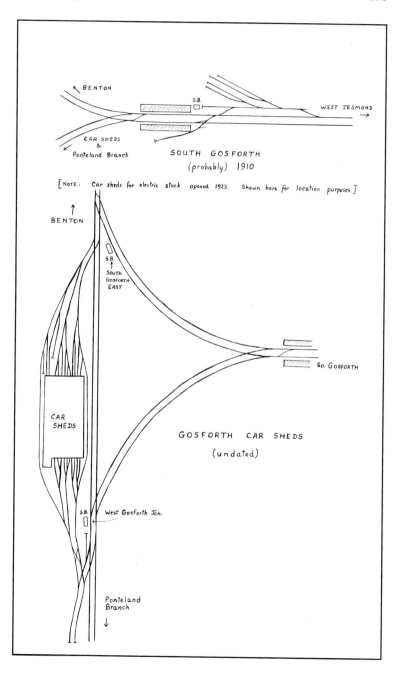

← BENTON

S.B.

WEST JESMOND →

CAR SHEDS
&
Ponteland Branch

SOUTH GOSFORTH
(probably) 1910

[NOTE: Car sheds for electric stock opened 1923. Shown here for location purposes.]

↑
BENTON

S.B.
↑
SOUTH
GOSFORTH
EAST

So. GOSFORTH

CAR
SHEDS

GOSFORTH CAR SHEDS
(undated)

S.B. West Gosforth Jcn. ←

Ponteland
Branch
↓

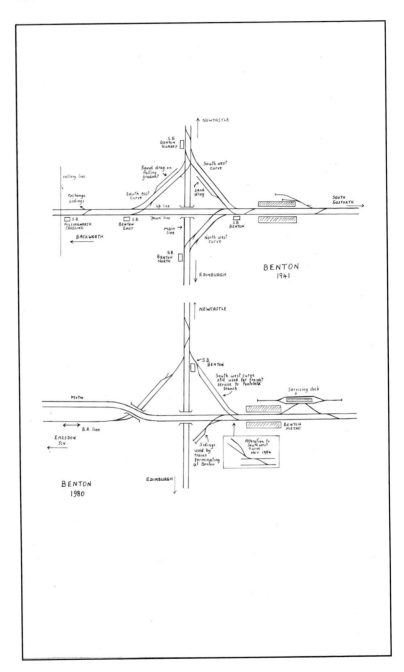

BENTON
1941

BENTON
1980

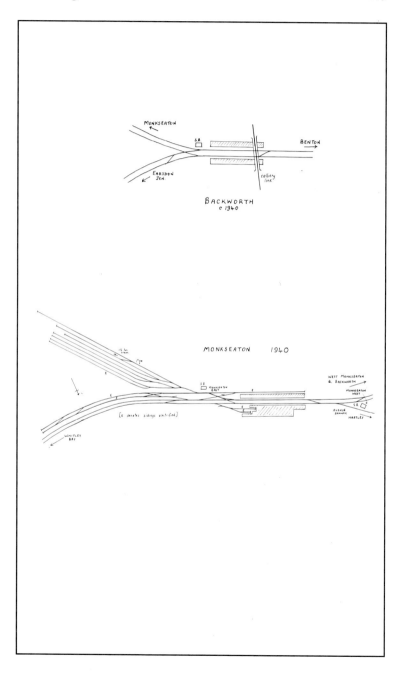

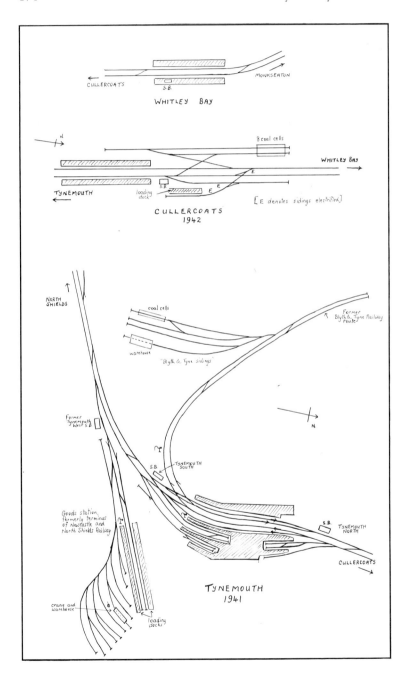

CULLERCOATS
WHITLEY BAY

MONKSEATON

S.B.

WHITLEY BAY

N

8 coal cells

TYNEMOUTH

loading
dock

E

E

E

WHITLEY BAY

[E denotes sidings electrified]

CULLERCOATS
1942

NORTH
SHIELDS

coal cells

warehouse

Former
Blyth & Tyne Railway
route

'Blyth & Tyne sidings'

Former
Tynemouth
West S.B.

N

Goods station,
formerly Terminus
of Newcastle and
North Shields Railway

S.B.

TYNEMOUTH
SOUTH

S.B.

TYNEMOUTH
NORTH

CULLERCOATS

crane and
warehouse

loading
docks

TYNEMOUTH
1941

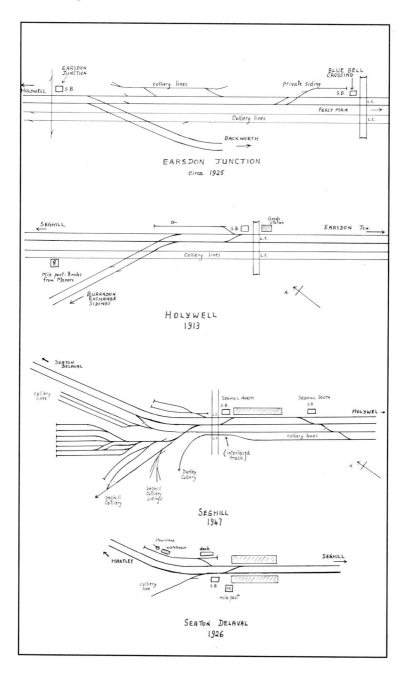

EARSDON JUNCTION
circa 1925

HOLYWELL
1913

SEGHILL
1947

SEATON DELAVAL
1926

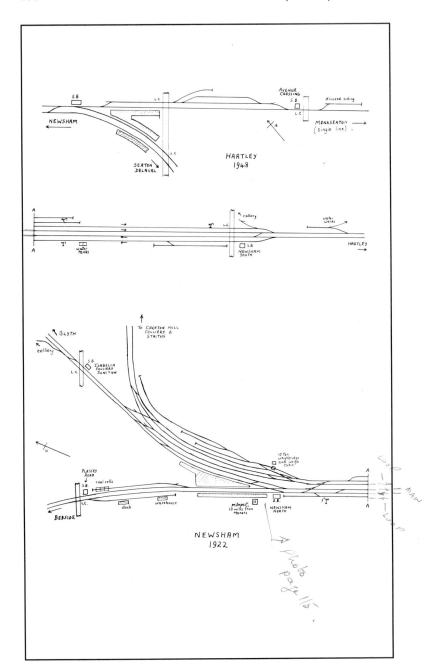

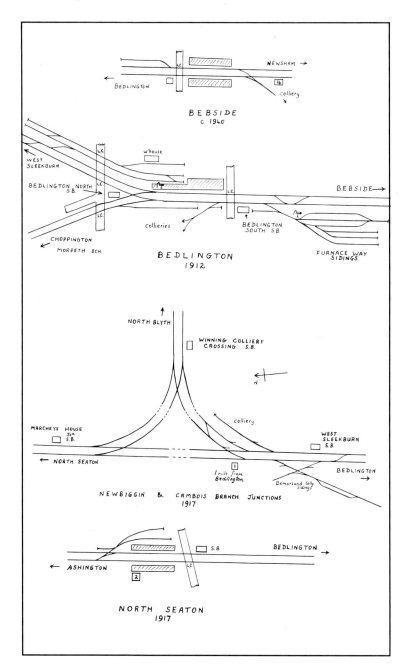

BEBSIDE
c 1940

BEDLINGTON
1912

NEWBIGGIN & CAMBOIS BRANCH JUNCTIONS
1917

NORTH SEATON
1917

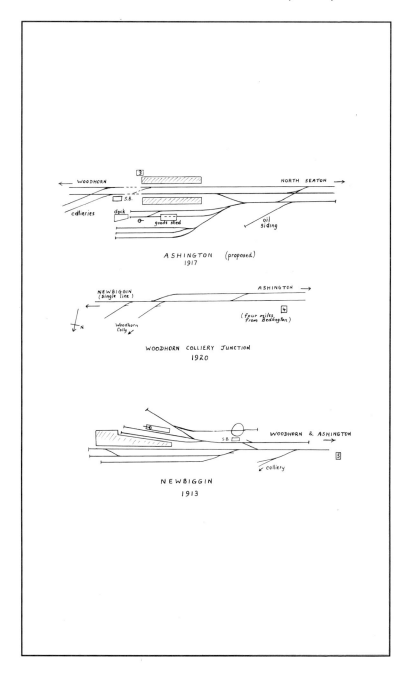

WOODHORN   NORTH SEATON

3

S.B.

collieries

deck

goods shed

oil
siding

ASHINGTON (proposed)
1917

NEWBIGGIN
(single line)   ASHINGTON

4

(four miles
from Bedlington)

N

Woodhorn
Colly

WOODHORN COLLIERY JUNCTION
1920

S.B.   WOODHORN & ASHINGTON

5

colliery

NEWBIGGIN
1913

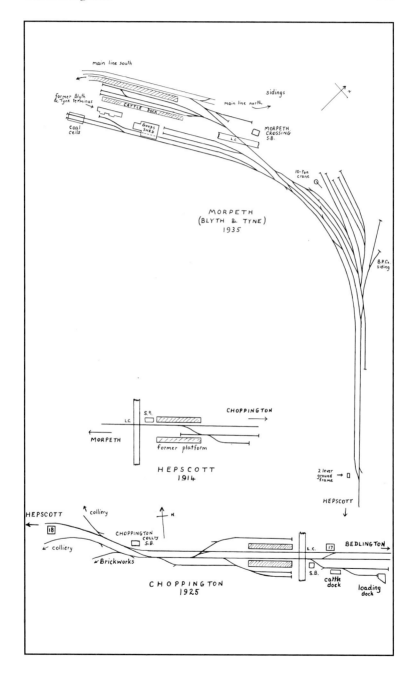

main line south

former Blyth
& Tyne terminus

CATTLE DOCK

sidings

main line north

Coal
cells

GOODS
SHED

MORPETH
CROSSING
S.B.

L.C.

10-ton
crane

MORPETH
(BLYTH & TYNE)
1935

B.P.Co.
siding

S.B.

CHOPPINGTON

L.C.

MORPETH

former platform

HEPSCOTT
1914

2 lever
ground
frame

HEPSCOTT

HEPSCOTT

colliery

N.

CHOPPINGTON
COLL'Y
S.B.

L.C.

17

BEDLINGTON

18

colliery

Brickworks

S.B.

cattle
dock

loading
dock

CHOPPINGTON
1925

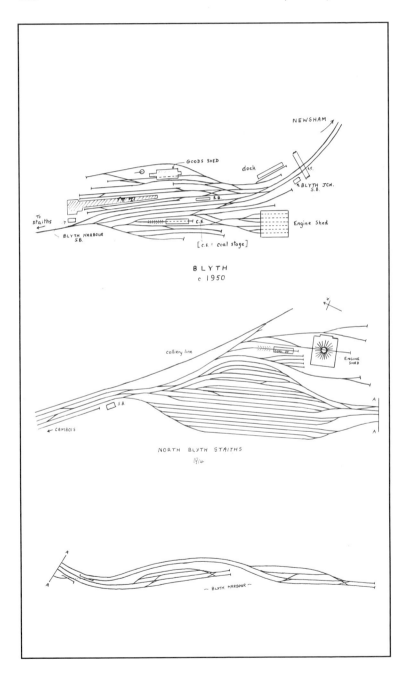

BLYTH
c 1950

[c.s. = coal stage]

NORTH BLYTH STAITHS
1914

~ BLYTH HARBOUR ~

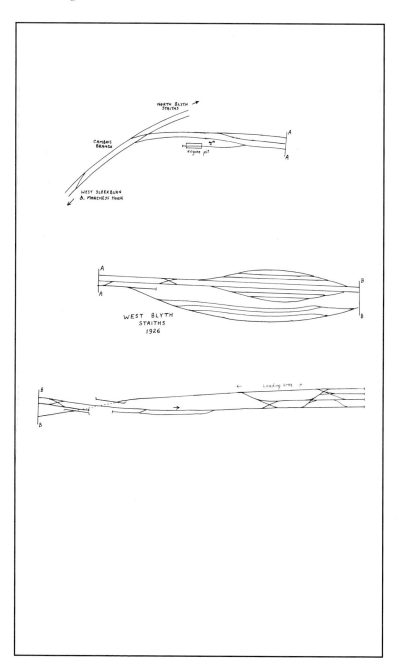

NORTH BLYTH
STAITHS

CAMBOIS
BRANCH

engine pit

A

A

WEST SLEEKBURN
& MARCHEYS HOUSE

A

A

B

B

WEST BLYTH
STAITHS
1926

B

B

Loading area

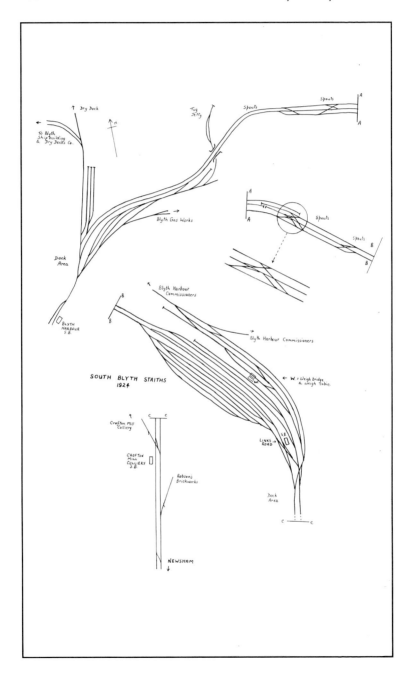

↖ To Blyth
Ship Building
& Dry Docks Co.

↑ Dry Dock

↑ N

Tug
Jetty

Spouts

Spouts

A
A

Blyth Gas Works →

A
A

→

Spouts

Dock
Area

A
A

Spouts

B
B

⬜ BLYTH
HARBOUR
S.B.

B
B

↑ Blyth Harbour
Commissioners

↑ Blyth Harbour Commissioners

SOUTH BLYTH STAITHS
1924

← W = Weigh bridge
& Weigh Cabin.

↑ Crofton Mill
Colliery

c   c

CROFTON
MILL
COLLIERY
S.B.

Robsons
Brickworks

LINKS →
ROAD   S.B.

Dock
Area

c   c

NEWSHAM
↓

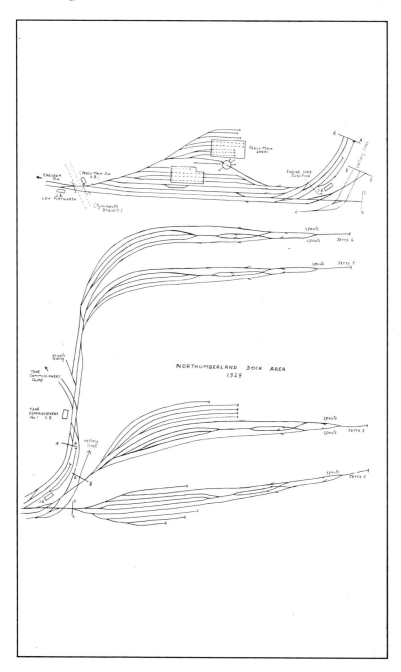

NORTHUMBERLAND DOCK AREA
1928

Principal Sources of Information

Blyth Harbour Commissioners: Clerk's Half Yearly Report, 1909.

British Rail: *Senior Staff* Messrs P Atack, K Dickens, G Robson. Letters in response to enquiries. Short Works Course for Public and Grammar School Boys, 1960. Traffic returns.

British Railways Magazine, August 1956: "Calling on You, Blyth".

Department of Transport Accident Reports (Morpeth, West Sleekburn).

Friends of Tynemouth Station: publicity sheet, 1987

Local Studies Centre, North Shields: newspaper reports.

Newcastle City Library, Local Studies Section: various newspaper reports, accident reports, etc.

North Eastern Railway Association: various articles in The *North Eastern Express,* particularly research by Messrs J C Dean, J M Fleming and J Mallon.

"The North Eastern Railway: Its Rise & Development" W W Tomlinson.

Northumberland County Library, Blyth Branch: newspaper reports.

Northumberland County Record Office: track plans, maps, documents; Seaton Delaval Council Minutes; Blyth Harbour papers.

Personal reminiscences.

Railwaymen, past and present.

Research by Messrs T Allan, M Charlton and the late J Scott.

Signal box Occurrence Books.

Stephenson Museum Project: information sheets and publicity material.

Traffic figures supplied by Mr J Sinclair, last Station Master at Newsham.

Tyne & Wear Transport Executive: news sheets and publicity material.

Bibliography

Allen, C J   The North Eastern Railway
                            Ian Allan Ltd. 1964

Baldwin, C E   The History & Development of the Port of Blyth
                            Andrew Reid & Co., Newcastle upon Tyne 1929

Bolger, Paul   BR Steam Motive Power Depots, NER
                            Ian Allan Ltd. 1984

Casserley, H C &   Locomotives at the Grouping, Vol 2 LNER
Johnson S W   Ian Allan Ltd. 1966

Cook, R A &   North Eastern Railway Historical Maps
Hoole, K   Railway & Canal Historical Society 1975

Crump, Norman   By Rail to Victory: The Story of the LNER in
                            Wartime. London & North Eastern Railway 1947

Foster, Colin   North Eastern Record
(Editor)   The Historical Model Railway Society 1988

Hoole, K   North Eastern Branch Lines Past & Present
                            Oxford Publishing Company 1984

Hoole, K   Newcastle (Rail Centres) Ian Allan Ltd. 1986

                            Railways of Tyneside: A Pictorial History
                            compiled by K Hoole
                            Dalesman Publications 1983
Hoole, K   The North Eastern Electrics (The History of
                            Tyneside Passenger Services, 1904-1967)
                            Oakwood Press 1987

Joyce, James   Roads & Rails of Tyne & Wear, 1900-1980
                            Ian Allan Ltd. 1985

Maclean, J S   Locomotives of the North Eastern Railway,
                      1854-1905
                      R Robinson & Co., Newcastle upon Tyne 1905

Tomlinson, W W   The North Eastern Railway, Its Rise &
                      Development
                      Andrew Reid, Newcastle upon Tyne 1915
                      David & Charles, 3rd Edition, 1987

Tuplin, W A   North Eastern Steam
                      George Allen & Unwin Ltd. 1970

White, Horace   Battleship Wharf
                      Published privately by Hughes Bolckow Ltd.
                      1961
Williams, F S   Our Iron Roads, Their History, Construction
                      and Social Influence
                      Bemrose & Sons, London 4th Edition, 1883.

Some dates of interest mentioned in the text

1874   The Blyth & Tyne Railway became part of the North Eastern Railway.

1878.   Hirst Station opened. (Renamed Ashington in 1889.)

1879   South Blyth engine sheds opened. (Enlarged 1895.)

1880   Blyth & Tyne Branch trains began using the main station at Morpeth.

1882   New line opened nearer the coast. New stations at Whitley, Cullercoats and Tynemouth.

1884   Staiths at Low Quay, South Blyth, opened.

1886   Ashington Colliery complex joined to the North Eastern Railway at Hirst station.

1888   New Blyth staiths opened.

1889-90 NER constructed almost 60 breakdown trains.

1894   Class 0 0-4-4 tank engines (G5) introduced by the NER.

1896   Rebuilding of Blyth station completed.
        Line opened between Marcheys House and Winning.
        Staiths in use at North Blyth.
        Clerestory coaches being built in large numbers.

1897   North Blyth engine shed opened.

1899   The new Whitley station renamed Whitley Bay.

1900   Flood at Newsham station.

1902   20-ton trucks introduced as standard coal wagons.

1903   40-ton coal wagons in use between Ashington and Blyth.
        Benton south west curve opened.

1904   Electric trains commenced running on Blyth & Tyne route to the coast.
        Passenger trains restored to Avenue branch.
        Benton south east curve opened.
        NER goods engines appeared in black livery.

1906   P3 0-6-0 locomotives (J27) introduced by the NER.

1907   New Bridge Street Goods Station in part use.

1908   New Bridge Street terminus closed to passenger traffic.

1909   Link between Jesmond and the main line at Manors.
        New station at Manors.

	Over 500 fishing boats using Blyth.
	Benton Square station opened. (Closed 1915.)
1910	New station at Whitley Bay built alongside old one.
	First fish train ran from Blyth.
1913	Over 10 million passengers carried on North Tyneside electric trains.
1914	Line laid from Avenue Branch to Collywell Bay, Seaton Sluice.
1915	New station opened at Monkseaton.
1916	Hughes Bolckow (Blyth) commenced breaking up *Britannia*, the largest 3-deck sailing ship ever built.
1917	All electric trains started from and terminated at Newcastle Central.
1918	Electric car sheds at Walkergate destroyed by fire.
1923	Grouping. The NER formed part of the London & North Eastern Railway.
	New electric car sheds at South Gosforth.
	Two locomen killed in accident at South Gosforth.
1928	West staiths completed at Blyth.
	Royal Train at Jesmond.
1933	West Monkseaton station opened.
	Exhibition of locomotives and rolling stock at Blyth.
1937	New electric trains began running on Blyth & Tyne line to Tynemouth.
1940	Benton north west curve opened.
1941	New Bridge Street warehouse badly damaged in air raid.
1947	Longbenton station opened to serve Ministry of National Insurance.
1948	Railways nationalised and became British Railways.
1950	Passenger traffic withdrawn between Bedlington and Morpeth.
1956-57	Colour-light signalling installed at Newcastle.
1958	Newcastle handled 14,665,968 passengers: the highest of any station outside London.
1959	Goods traffic withdrawn from Tynemouth.
1961	Blyth became Europe's busiest coal-handling port.
1963	Blyth closed to goods traffic.
1964	Passenger services on Blyth & Tyne Branch withdrawn north of Backworth.
	Newcastle signal box took over working of Manors,

Jesmond and West Jesmond.

1965	Percy Main motive power depot closed to steam.
1967	South Blyth motive power depot closed (May):
	North Blyth motive power depot closed (September).
	Last electric trains ran from Newcastle.
	Test runs of merry-go-round trains.
1968	Cambois diesel depot opened.
	Construction commenced of smelter at Lynemouth.
1972	Blyth station demolished.
1975	Prototype Metrocars on test at Middle Engine Lane.
1977	Backworth station closed.
1978	Jesmond, West Jesmond, South Gosforth, Longbenton and Benton stations closed to prepare for Metro.
	New signal box at Morpeth.
1979	West Monkseaton, Monkseaton, Whitley Bay and Cullercoats stations closed.
1980	First section of Metro opened on former Blyth & Tyne route, between Haymarket and Tynemouth.
	Blyth & Tyne Branch connected to main line north of Morpeth.
1989	West staiths, Blyth, closed.
	Coal, alumina and aluminium only traffic on Blyth & Tyne Branch.
	Blyth & Tyne sidings at Morpeth used as depot for electrification of east coast main line.

Some Railway terms used on the Blyth & Tyne Branch

ADVANCE
: The home signal controlling entry into the next section, usually situated beyond a signal box.

ATTACH
: Used when a vehicle or vehicles are joined to a train.

BACKBOARD
: A small light at the rear of a semaphore signal to enable a signalman know the signal is lit when it faces away from him. The light is concealed when the signal is in the 'off' position.

BAY PLATFORM
: (or simply bay) One which does not have a through line but ends with a buffer stop.

BLOCK SECTION
: Basically, the line or lines between two connected signal boxes.

BLOW
: (appertaining to steam locomotives) to use the whistle.

BLOW OFF
: The release of steam through the safety valve.

BOARD
: A semaphore signal. The origin of this was the early type of mechanical signal, a circular board.

BOGIES
: Small four or six-wheeled 'trucks' on which the bodies of coaches and long wagons are pivoted and supported to give easier running. (Some special wagons for carrying very heavy loads had either more wheels in each pair of bogies or, in some cases, several bogies to spread the weight.)

BRAKEY
: An express goods, milk, fish, livestock, etc train in which all the vehicles conform to coaching stock standards (qv), the majority, or all, being braked from the engine.

CALLER
: A junior employee sent round to houses of drivers, firemen, etc to call or knock them up for duty during the night or early morning.

CHAIR
: Metal fixing on sleepers to support rails.

CLEAR
: Signal or signals in the 'off' position.

CLOSE COUPLED
: Vehicles held close together by a screw coupling, buckeye or similar device.

COACHING-
: Vehicles intended to travel at higher speeds

STOCK STANDARDS	had to have a minimum 9 ft wheelbase, brakes capable of being worked from the locomotive, screw couplings and long buffers.
COUPLE UP	Join locomotives/coaches/wagons together.
CRACKERS	(also *bangers*) Detonators.
CRIPPLE	A locomotive, coach or wagon which has been damaged and cannot be used in normal service, or which is unfit to run for other reasons.
CROW	A steam engine whistle code consisting of one, pause, two, pause, two toots (1-2-2). Two crows was used as a signal to start when an engine was used as a banker at the rear of a train.
DETACH	Take engine off train or shunt off coaches or wagons.
DISTANT	A signal which tells a driver whether the signals in the section ahead are clear or at danger.
DOCKIE	Notices for enginemen posted in a motive power depot.
DOLLY	A ground signal used for shunting purposes.
DOG AND MONKEY	A nickname given by signalmen in the Morpeth area to the Leeds-Glasgow express. (Origin not known).
EMPTIES	Usually applied to empty coal or mineral wagons but may be used for any empty wagons.
EX	From.
FAST	Stuck. (*Examples:* The train could not leave because the points were fast. The engine was fast in the snow drift.)
FAST, The	An express passenger train, hence "The fast is due through in ten minutes."
FITTED WAGON	One with brakes which can be worked from the locomotive.
FOREIGN	Rolling stock which belongs to a different company. (Pre-nationalisation or pre-grouping.)
FOUR-FOOT	The gauge of railway lines is 4ft 8½ ins which is the distance between the rails. For brevity it is referred to as the four-foot.
FULLY FITTED FREIGHT	An express goods train in which all the vehicles conform to coaching stock standards and all, or most, are braked from the engine.

GAFFER	Person in charge: the boss.
GANGER	Leader of a gang of platelayers.
GLASS CARRIAGE	An Officers' Special, used to convey senior railway officials. The saloon had fairly large windows, hence the name.
GO QUIETLY	Proceed slowly. (An engine which is not having to work hard runs more quietly!)
HANDLAMP	A hand lamp which can show three aspects - white, green or red.
HAP-UP	A heavy snow fall.
INDEPENDENT	A line longer than a 'loop' which runs alongside a main line or running line and normally takes slower-moving traffic.
INSTANTER	A type of three-link coupling which can be used in the long or short position.
JACKS	Safety points.
KEYS	Wooden chocks for holding rails firmly in the chairs.
LIFT, The	The act of lifting with (usually) a breakdown crane.
LIFT, To	A term used when a locomotive starts its train. (The engine had difficulty in lifting the heavy train.)
LIGHT ENGINE	(or running light) A locomotive running on its own or with not more than two brake vans attached.
LOOP	A section of track alongside another with points at both ends enabling, for example, a locomotive to run round its train.
LOOSE COUPLED	Wagons or vans joined by the standard three-link couplings.
LOWP ON HINNY	(NB. The 'low-' rhymes with cow.) An exhortation used by some porters to encourage passengers to join a train!
MARSHALL	Sorting coaches or wagons to make up a train.
OFF THE ROAD	A derailment.
ON/OFF	The position of a signal showing stop, proceed with caution, or all clear.
ON THE BLOCK	Indication on a block instrument that a train is approaching.

PATH	Planned movement times for a train over a particular route. (A train running late might lose its path and be subject to more delays.)
PICK WHEELS UP	An expression used when the driving wheels of a locomotive are not in normal contact with the rails such as in a wheel-slip or skid.
PILOT	(i) An additional engine assisting at the front of a train. (ii) A local, or pick-up, goods train.
PIN BRAKES DOWN	On a freight train not braked from the engine it was sometimes necessary to stop at the top of a gradient so that some wagon brakes could be put on to assist the loco in the descent. The brake levers could be held in various positions by a steel pin.
POINTS	Where lines converge or diverge.
POWS	Privately owned wagons, referring particularly to coal traffic pre-1948.
PULL OFF	The use of levers in a signal box which pull wires to change signals to the clear or 'off' position.
PUT INSIDE	To clear a main line or other running line by putting a train into a loop or siding to enable another train to pass.
RAMPS	Heavy metal objects used to put wheels of wagons back on the track after a simple derailment.
ROAD, The	Simply, the railway track. 'Given the road' means given the signals to proceed along the track. 'Off the road' is a derailment.
RUN ROUND	To transfer the engine from one end of a train to the other. 'A run round' may be used to describe a short loop for the same purpose.
SANDS	Dry sand was applied to wet railway lines to help locos grip the track. The lever for doing this was called *the sands*. Sometimes these words were used to denote the sand boxes on the engine and the pipes leading from them. Larger passenger and freight engines used steam instead of sand.
SCREW COUPLING	A coupling which can be tightened to hold vehicles closer together.

SET	On the Blyth & Tyne Branch this usually referred to a train of coal wagons but could also be used for passenger coaches, especially those kept together for a period.
SHOPS	Workshops where locomotives and rolling stock were repaired.
SHUNT	Sorting wagons or coaches: making up or breaking up trains: attaching or detaching.
SIDE LAMP	The brake van of an 'unfitted' goods or mineral train carried a lamp on each side near the roof which showed red to the rear and white to the front at night. The white lights could be seen by the driver who then knew his train was complete. The brake van also carried a tail lamp lower down, thus the three lights formed a triangle.
SIDING	A length of track ending in buffer stops where coaches and wagons are stored or where wagons are loaded or unloaded.
SIGNALMAN'S FAREWELL	The bell code for closing of signal box (7-5-5).
SIX-FOOT	The space between adjacent tracks.
SLACKED	Slowed down. The driver of a loose-coupled train would reduce speed if he saw a distant signal at caution. Doing so would slacken the couplings.
SLIP	Wheel-spin on a wet rail as an engine tries to lift its load.
SLOW, The	A stopping passenger train.
STRENGTHEN	Adding more coaches to a train.
STUCK	Unable to move.
TAIL LAMP	A lamp or light at the end of a train (red at night) showing signalmen that the train is complete.
TANKIE	A tank engine.
TEDDY BEAR	The name given to Gresley's V1/V3 2-6-2 tank engines.
TENDER FIRST	An engine running with its tender leading, as opposed to 'chimney first'. A tank engine, which does not have a separate tender, was said to be running chimney first or *bunker* first.
THROUGH PLATFORM	A platform built alongside part of a continuous line.

TOOL VANS   Breakdown train.
TRAIN DIVIDED   A train which has broken into two or more parts,
                    unintentionally.
UNFITTED   (i) A freight train where the vehicles are not
                    braked from the engine.
                    (ii) A single wagon or van with no continuous
                    brake, having hand brakes only.

Index